8/25/13

BROKEN PROMISES:

Whatever happened to Vatican Council II?

The Catholic hierarchy's failure to follow through on the mandate of Vatican Council II to open up the Church is the most critical missed opportunity for the Church in contemporary times. The cover-up by the hierarchy of pedophile priests is most damaging and threatens the very survival of our Church. Our hopes are now focused on the "People of God" calling for Vatican Council III to save Catholicism.

Finbarr M Corr Ed. D.

Trafford rev. 03/22/2012

 www.trafford.com

North America & international
toll-free: 1 888 232 4444 (USA & Canada)
phone: 250 383 6864 ♦ fax: 812 355 4082

CONTENTS

DEDICATION AND ACKNOWLEDGEMENTS

This book is the result of serving twenty-eight years in the priesthood of a Church that I love. I was fortunate to meet some of the Church's finest bishops, priests, religious and laity as I served the faithful of the Paterson Diocese during the pre-Vatican era, the Council (1962-65) and beyond. Some of those men and women are already in heaven enjoying the Beatific Vision. Some of the popes that I never met, except through my several years of research for this book . . . like Pope John XXIII, have left an indelible mark on my soul and have motivated me to write this book.

I am of course saddened by what has happened, and is still happening, to our beloved Church because of the failure of the Church hierarchy to live up to the promises made by the Council Fathers during Vatican Council II. I am however hopeful, as you will read in these twenty-seven chapters. Church leaders, like Archbishop Diarmuid Martin of Dublin, Cardinal Sean O'Malley of Boston and Bishop Liam McDaid of the Diocese of Clogher in Monaghan, who put the healing of victims of pedophile priests before protecting the good name of the Church have earned the respect of all of us who want to heal our broken church and reform Catholicism.

I am grateful to the Catholic Priests Association and the People of God in Ireland and other reform groups in the US and Europe. To these reformers and the prelates listed above I dedicate *Broken Promises: Whatever happened to Vatican Council II?*

I am indebted to my wife Laurie for her patience and support over the past two and one-quarter years as I researched, wrote and rewrote this book. I thank Marge Frith from our Wednesday Writers Group on Cape Cod for her editing and Elizabeth Moisan for her unique sketch of Cardinal O'Malley.

I am grateful to my classmate Monsignor Patrick Scott, who traveled the same journey through two St. Patrick's Colleges in Cavan and Carlow to serve with me in the Diocese of Paterson, New Jersey. Thanks, Pat, for your endorsement. Thank you also to Dr. Anthony Padovano and Tom O'Connell for their affirming endorsements and to Father Tom Doyle for his encouraging support.

PREFACE

What happened over the three years of the Second Vatican Council, convened by Pope John XXIII on October 11, 1962? One Irish archbishop arriving home from the fourth and last session in 1965 declared "NOTHING." But was that accurate? Was nothing accomplished, even by the sixteen documents on liturgy, ecumenism, social communication and religious liberty that were created by participants at the Council? According to author James Carroll, expectations were high and the aims were lofty: the Council was "the Church's great attempt to deal more honestly with the contradiction between a religious culture still firmly rooted in the Middle Ages and a Catholic people who had come of age in the modern world."[1]

Pope John XXIII surprised the Catholic world when he suddenly declared the need to convene the Council in a vibrant spirit of openness. He proclaimed, "It is not that the Gospel has changed: it is that we have begun to understand it better. . . . [We] know that the moment has come to discern the signs of the times, to seize the opportunity and to look far ahead." This pope, whose multi-faceted and multi-cultural path to the papacy began very simply and humbly in a small Italian country village, was uniquely qualified to understand why the Church needed to change if it was to retain its relevance in the world.

As a result of the Council, Catholic attitudes towards liturgy and theology shifted dramatically. Interreligious dialogue advanced among Christians and between Christians and Jews. The Church questioned its own exercise of power and invited the laity to become more active in

Church life and community. Pope John XXIII trusted his fellow bishops and the Catholic people to bring about such basic changes. The tragedy is that Pope John died in 1963 when the Council's work was barely underway. What a different Catholic Church we would experience today if Pope John XXIII had lived!

Vatican Council II's call for reform may once have been arbitrary in some people's minds, but it no longer can be so. The need to complete the reform the Council promised is now urgent. The "cancer" of sexual abuse of children by priests and the related cover-up by the hierarchy have accelerated an ever-growing cascade of Church crises, questioning and near-revolt, even in countries with deep-rooted Catholic traditions such as Ireland.

The Council's promise is not fully realized, its work not yet finished. This book examines the ongoing conflict between the top-down, authoritative model of Church administration and the bottom-up, democratic model that Pope John XXIII envisioned for the renewed People of God, a priesthood whereby the laity would openly share with the ministerial priesthood in both Church administration and discernment about the Church's role in the context of modern society.

By reviewing different countries and cultures where Catholicism has been practiced for centuries, the discussion explores the roles and backgrounds of popes, cardinals and bishops as the drama has played out worldwide. The book attempts to provide valuable perspective about the key forces and influences on Church leaders so that readers can judge the situation for themselves.

Is there still hope for a Church now marred by such egregious abuse and cover-up, a Church locked up by its "closed-door" policy? Can the Church still effectively live up to its mission of ministering to the poor and underprivileged and remain a respected leader in standards of reverence for life on earth?

Change from the bottom up has begun. Catholics are gathering spontaneously to address a range of critical moral and administrative problems. The motto of the reform group Voice of the Faithful speaks for many Catholics as they work respectfully to "KEEP THE FAITH, CHANGE THE CHURCH."

The Church is not its church buildings but is, in reality, only living stones, its people, who are "called out of darkness into His wonderful light" to save it (Peter 2:8-9). Vatican III, or whatever its organizers may choose to call it, *must* come and *must* involve the priesthood of the laity working as equals with the ministerial priesthood for reform to be authentic. Only this united force will give the Church its best chance of discerning where the Holy Spirit is leading the People of God so that all who are seeking may follow.

(Some paragraphs and words in the book are printed in italics for emphasis).

CHAPTER I

Vatican Council II: A Surprise

I arrived at his rectory door at 11:58 on that July morning in 1962. He was waiting in the living room, dressed in full clericals, with a white straw hat and a black patch covering his left eye. The noon church bell rang as I entered. He grinned and said, "You just made it." Father Michael Corr, my dad's brother, expected people to be on time. On Sunday mornings he dressed in his vestments and sat in meditation, waiting for the clock to strike ten before starting the procession to Mass.

I loved the man. He exemplified my motivation to become a priest. I learned from him when I drove him through the hills of Sussex County, New Jersey. He was a country pastor there in the years after his service with distinction as a U.S. Army chaplain during the First World War. He could no longer drive, having lost the sight in his eye to cancer. Yet his capacity for speaking his mind was undiminished.

In the early sixties my dear uncle loved to say, "Thank God I am an old man, as I will probably die Catholic" (meaning a pre-Vatican II conservative Catholic). I chose not to answer him. I needed his support and also didn't want to think of him ever dying.

I thank God that he is not around today. He would be appalled over the challenges his beloved Church now faces: Catholics deserting the pews on Sunday morning; the critical shortage of priests; a Church hierarchy shielding pedophile priests from justice to protect the good name of the Church, while ignoring the trauma caused to thousands of children sexually abused by priests. Father Michael's Church is on the precipice of disaster.

Father Michael was comfortable serving in a hierarchical organization where all instructions and inspiration come from the top. He welcomed the aging Angelo Giuseppe Roncalli as the new pope in October 1958. But he was not happy when Roncalli, the "stop-gap" Pope John XXIII, announced three months later on January 25, 1959, that a Council would be convened, saying, "It is time to open the windows of the Church and let in some fresh air."[1]

Angelo Roncalli didn't campaign to be elected pope, and he never expected the honor. He enjoyed being just a priest. He and his secretary had round-trip railroad tickets in their pockets as they arrived in Rome for the papal election in 1958. When he was elected, Roncalli surprised all of his fellow cardinals by choosing the name John XXIII, the name of an antipope who reigned from 1410 to 1415 during the Western Schism.

He announced, "I choose John . . . a name sweet to us because it is the name of our father, dear to me because it is the name of the humble parish church where I was baptized, the solemn name of cathedrals throughout the world, including our own basilica [St. John Lateran]. Twenty-two Johns of indisputable legitimacy [have been] pope and almost all of them have had a brief pontificate. We have preferred to hide the smallness of our name behind the magnificent succession of Roman Popes."[2] In choosing the name John XXIII, he affirmed the antipapal status of antipope John XXIII.

This particular pope captured the affection of millions of Catholics and non-Catholics all over the world. The combination of his personal warmth, good sense of humor and the ability to see himself as a servant priest has no equal among his predecessors or successors. He pleasantly surprised many Catholics around the world with his news of the Second Vatican Council.

Father Michael, and many of his conservative friends, didn't see the need for a Council. He would ask, "Why is it necessary to drag all the cardinals and bishops of the world to Rome away from their dioceses to do what . . . listen to theological experts who don't know how to run a diocese or a parish?"

"Uncle Michael, many forward-thinking Catholics are happy about the possibilities of such a Council. In anticipation of the liturgical changes that a Council may bring, progressive organizations like the Christian Family Movement are holding private masses recited in English in their basements, and missionaries in Africa are introducing tribal dances into their liturgies."

"I can tell whose side you are on," he muttered, ending our conversation about the Council for that day.

Traditionally, only bishops and cardinals participated in ecumenical Councils. Pope John XXIII broke with tradition by involving progressive theologians called *periti* (experts). Among them were Karl Rahner from Germany and American John Courtney Murray (both members of the Society of Jesus, the Jesuits), with several others to give insight into the Body of Christ, the name Pope John liked to call his Church. Breaking further with tradition, he invited leaders of Protestant and Orthodox churches to observe the historical debates. Several Protestant denominations and Eastern churches sent acceptances. The one major disappointment at this stage of the Council was that, although there were nearly three thousand invitees, Pope John did not invite any women to participate.

Preparation for the Council took more than two years and received no press in the public media. The Catholic press prepared the laity for some of the possible changes, such as alterations to the Liturgy. Conservative Catholic papers like the *Wanderer* put the news of the Council in the middle or towards the back of their paper, while the progressive *National Catholic Reporter* featured it as "Good News" on the front page. I have fond memories of the feelings of hope and excitement that progressive Catholics experienced.

Other more distinguished authors like Archbishop Rembert G. Weakland of Milwaukee wrote, "An important part of that history was how the council was received; it changed how many saw the future of the Church, igniting and fanning positive hopes and aspirations." Then he added, "The very person of Pope John XXIII, his attitude towards an all-inclusive Church, his positive assessment of the world, his love of the human person, his quest for peace, his inward tranquility and his sense of humor all added to the excitement."[3]

Pope John knew that the Church would now be described as all-inclusive. He addressed all Catholics, including the laity, when he said, "I want the Council to increase the fervor and energy of Catholics, to serve the needs of Christian people." He purposefully said the needs of "Christian" people, not just Catholic people. The pope directed the statement primarily to bishops and priests, encouraging them to grow in holiness, and then to the laity, moving them to learn more about their faith. He then exhorted the entire adult Catholic community to make adequate provision to educate their children holistically.

As one pilgrim who has spent several months in the Eternal City, I admired the Italian preacher's unique expressive gestures, waving his arms over the congregation like the *Polizia Stradale* directing traffic on Via Vittorio Veneto, Roma. I can see the big happy Italian pope gesturing with outstretched arms exclaiming, *"Aggiornamento,"* meaning that the Church must be brought forward to adapt itself to the challenges of modern times. He pushed open the papal windows overlooking St. Peter's Square to let in some fresh air. If only my dear uncle, Father Michael, were there to witness it. The papal household, called the *Curia*, didn't watch. They were scared; they felt their power over the Catholic world being swept out the window.

A political party in the United States does not run and hide if they lose the majority in the Senate to the other party in a national election. No, they fight back with filibusters and they start campaigning, determined to win the elections four years hence. The *Curia* did not relinquish its power over the Catholic Church worldwide, handing the reins over to bishops in third world countries and theologians, some of who were unknown to the *Curia* members before 1962. They were frightened at the possibility of the Holy Spirit, now let loose in the Council chambers, guiding not only Pope John XXIII, but also cardinals, bishops, and, in their minds, "crazy" theologians to, God forbid, ordain women and married men to the priesthood.

The *Curia* recoiled in shock during the first session on October 13, 1962, when they tried to rush the first item on the agenda (i.e., election of the ten Council commissions), hoping their members who served on the preparatory commission would be confirmed and thus be the majority on the several commissions. Cardinal Lienart, from Paris, objected, "We do not accept this way of doing things. We ask for forty-eight hours to reflect, that we might know better those who could make up the different commissions." German Cardinal Frings seconded Lienart's proposal.[4] The Curia learned on the first day that they were not in charge, which added to their paranoia of losing power. That first session on October 13 lasted fifteen minutes.

As the discussions continued in the second session, the celebration of the Mass was given the highest priority. The new document *Constitution on the Sacred Liturgy, Sacrosanctum Concilium* declared: "Every liturgical celebration, because it is an action of Christ the Priest and of his body which is the Church, is a sacred action surpassing all others. No other action of the Church can equal its efficacy by the same title and to the same degree" (*SC* 1).[5]

Progressive lay Catholics, when they attended Mass each Sunday, watched the priest facing the altar and muttering prayers in a language (Latin) they didn't understand. Instead of "wasting time" these Catholics took out their rosary beads and prayed to Mary. The only solution was a renewal of the Liturgy. Thus *Sacrosanctum Concilium* stipulated that "in this restoration both texts and rites should be drawn up so that they express more clearly the holy things which they signify; the Christian people, as far as possible, should be enabled to understand with ease and take part in this fulfilling activity and as befits their community" (*SC* 3).

The readings and prayers of the Mass were now translated into each country's native language. Experimentation in the Liturgy, while not encouraged, was accepted if it integrated the culture and traditions of the native people. The bishops of Africa and the Middle East welcomed the renewal and, in particular, the permission to experiment. If the experimental program was successful, the bishop was then required to apply to the *Congregation for the Sacred Liturgy* for approval. Progressive theologians objected to the centralization of power, demanding that cultural changes in the Liturgy needed Vatican approval.

The tension between the *Curia* and progressive Fathers of the Council, which was obvious on the very first day of the opening session, subsided; and discussions on the liturgical renewal, mass communication and relationships with Eastern Churches proceeded without further conflict. The same cannot be said when the Fathers initiated a discussion of the *Dogmatic Constitution on Divine Revelation, Dei Verbum*. The tension returned, and the prepared schema was rejected by the majority of the bishops. Pope John requested that it be rewritten, but he didn't live to see it completed. The Fathers finally approved it on November 11, 1965, long after his death on June 3, 1963.

The election of Cardinal Giovanni Battista Montini on June 21, 1963, as the next pope was not a surprise. He was thought of as progressive by many because of his friendship with all Christian churches, Muslims, atheists, and others. He did not possess Pope John's charm and warmth. The moderate and progressive arm of the Church felt confident that he would continue the modernization of the Church initiated by Pope John XXIII; he had announced at his coronation as Pope Paul VI that the Council would continue. This progressive assessment was not a true reflection of his theological stance. Although he and Roncalli had been good friends when Roncalli was Patriarch of Venice, when it was announced on January 25, 1959, that Roncalli as pope had called an ecumenical council, the then-Cardinal Montini said, "The holy old boy doesn't realize what a hornet's nest he's stirring up."[6]

In a radio address, Pope Paul VI recalled the uniqueness of his predecessors—"the strength of Pius XI," "the wisdom and intelligence of Pius XII," and "the love of John XXIII." He also highlighted his own pontifical goals, which included revising Canon Law, achieving peace and justice in the world, and uniting Christian Churches. This was one of John XXIII's primary goals.

Pope Paul VI reopened the Council, starting the second session on September 29, 1963. He initiated some reorganization to correct some of the problems that had surfaced during the first session. He invited additional lay Catholics and non-Catholic as observers. He surprised everybody by eliminating the requirement of secrecy of the discussions during the general sessions. As he welcomed the Fathers from all over the world to the second session, he listed his four priorities:

1. To understand the Church better. He reminded the Fathers not to create a new theology regarding the nature of the Church, as Pope Pius XII had already done this adequately in his encyclical

Mystici Corporis (Mystical Body), but to explain the Church in simple terms that the laity would understand.

2. To renew the Church. This involved a dialogue regarding the role of bishops, the laity and their relationship to the pope as leader of the Catholic world.

3. To restore Christian Unity. He apologized for any contribution that the Vatican had made to the separation.

4. To initiate a dialogue with the world, as he himself had created as archbishop of Milan. He invited the Fathers to seek contact with people from all walks of life.

Under the leadership of a younger, hands-on pope, the Council Fathers approved the *Constitution on the Sacred Liturgy, Sacrosanctum Concilium* and also the *Decree on the Means of Social Communication, Inter Mirifica,* a document about how local dioceses should communicate with the world. While discussing the role of bishops in the Church and steps toward Christian Unity, the *Curia* pushed to retain the status quo. Meanwhile, progressive bishops focused on the *aggiornamento* of open windows, transparency in Church governmental decisions and legislation, and making the Church more relevant to the modern world.

During one of the heated debates, Joseph Cardinal Frings criticized the Holy Office, which in turn drew an impassioned defense from the office of Secretary Alfred Cardinal Ottaviani. This was the most dramatic exchange during the whole Council.

I continued taking my aging uncle, Father Michael, for drives in the countryside. He retained his soldier's gait, walking with square shoulders and a brisk step. We both enjoyed seeing the change of seasons in Sussex County, New Jersey. We got into some lively discussions over dinner, many times on the subject of the Council. I was surprised when he and his associate pastors adapted the liturgical changes to include congregational singing. I'm not sure if his change was because the instructions were coming from the hierarchy above him or because of his own change of heart.

I enjoyed teasing him, saying, "Uncle, don't you think that the Council Fathers should engage more women in the discussions at the Council?" I will leave it to the reader to figure out his reply.

CHAPTER II

Vatican Council II: Effect on a Young Priest

I realized my goal of becoming a priest on June 11, 1960, barely a year after Pope John XXIII initiated the call for Vatican Council II to let in "some fresh air." The details of my first Mass on the following morning are still vivid in my mind. . . .

Mary Beatty, our family's former nanny and housekeeper, is sacristan and bell-ringer at St. Michael's. This is my childhood parish. Mary greets me with a hug, "Congratulations and best wishes Father Finbarr, I hope I have everything set up that you need for your first Mass."

"Everything looks fine. Thank you, Mary."

The Mass vestments are laid out atop the chest of drawers, exactly as she prepares them each morning for the pastor, Father McGauran. Mary is as excited and proud as my parents, Nell and John Frank, seated in the first pew, waiting for their seventh child to offer his first Holy Mass.

I experience a strange feeling in the sacristy that morning. While the altar boys light the altar candles and bring cruets of wine and water to the little side table, Mary is unusually quiet. She keeps looking at me and calling me "Father" Finbarr.

"Is there anything else I can do for you, Father Finbarr?"

"Not really Mary, I am nervous saying my first Mass before a church full of people." Mary remains silent.

A few days pass before I understand what actually happened that morning between Mary and me. In my mind, although now ordained, I am the same baby whose diapers she changed twenty-five years earlier in Legaginney House, our family's farm. But to Mary I am now a priest to be put on a pedestal and revered.

It is still the pre-Vatican II era, and one of the altar boys rings the bell. I walk in procession to the sanctuary with my brother, Father Jack, and his friend from New Jersey, Father Daly. There is no entrance hymn, and I don't face the people as I begin in Latin, saying, "*In nomine Patris, Filio et Spiritus Sancti.*" Other parts of the Mass—the Gloria, Oration, Epistle and Gospel—are all read in Latin. As a newly ordained priest, I am not expected to give a homily, or, as it was called back then, a "sermon." The first time I face the congregation is to distribute Holy Communion, beginning with my Mom and Dad. Mom smiles through her tears, while Dad, with eyes closed, opens his mouth to receive the bread that is the Body and Blood of Christ.

Mike-Joe Mulligan, Francie Corr, Toddy Maguire and Mel Lynch—all the local characters from the Lacken crossroads outside Lynch's shop—are there. They solemnly kneel to receive Holy Communion from the "new Father Finbarr." Later, as the ceremony ends, I give my first priestly blessing to all, beginning with my family. I solemnly say, "*Benedictio Dei omnipotenti, Patris, Filio et Spiritus Sancti descendat super Te et maneat semper.*"

When I come to Barney Brady, who accompanied me to parish dances while I was in college, I skip the Latin version. Instead I say, "May the blessing of almighty God, Father, Son and Holy Ghost descend on you, Barney, and remain with you forever," and I add, "Do you remember what you said to me six years ago when I told you I was going to be a priest? You said, "Oh, my God, Finbarr, it is going to be such a shock if you are ever ordained!" We both laugh.

This experience would have been different for all of us if the year were 1965 instead of 1960. The Mass (and hymns) would have been in English and celebrated facing the congregation, with both altar girls and boys. Girls were not yet considered suitable candidates to serve Mass, much less to celebrate Mass, in 1960.

Following a vacation with family and friends, in August of the same year I fly as a "missionary" priest to my new assignment at the inner-city parish of St. Agnes, Paterson, New Jersey. There I experience a typical pre-Vatican II pastor as my first boss. I will call him Monsignor X to protect his identity. Father Carl Wolsin, the "curate" (as associate pastors were called at the time) treats me as an equal. In contrast, when I ask the parish janitor for help on a project, Monsignor X, exercising the typical pastor-curate superiority, reminds me harshly, "The janitor was hired to serve me, not you," making me feel as if I committed a crime.

Wolsin, noticing my dejection, comes to my office to comfort me. "Finbarr, ignore him. He is just jealous of your popularity, with the Irish brogue and all that blarney. You are going to go places in this diocese, believe me."

"Thanks, Carl." That was affirmation I needed to hear.

Monsignor X is promoted to a larger parish. My brother Jack's best friend, Father Daly, becomes my pastor and boss. Three years before the Vatican Council urges collegiality among the priests and bishops, my new boss treats me as an equal.

We both enjoy working with lay volunteers in the parish and are not threatened by criticism. We laugh as Maggie Moran, a humorous volunteer, tells Father Daly at a pre-St. Patrick's celebration committee meeting, "We don't like stuffy priests here at St. Agnes Parish. You need to let your hair down."

Daly does not reply. He turns to me and says, "Wait until she sees and hears what I plan to do on St. Patrick's Night!" Father Daly shocks the entire parish that night when he dresses in costume along with Larry (the janitor), Gene, (an active volunteer), and me to mimic the Beatles singing "He loves you yeah, yeah, yeah."

As I look back now at that evening and remember the response of the 350 parishioners at the improvised concert, we were ready for the "opening of the windows of the Church, letting in the fresh air," as announced by the good Pope John XXIII. These experiences at the inner city parish were a positive preparation for the new initiative of *aggiornamento* soon launched by Pope John.

With a somewhat heavy heart, in July of 1966 I accept a transfer from this inner-city parish to St. Margaret's of Scotland, a suburban parish in Morristown, New Jersey. My new boss, Monsignor Christian D. Haag, calls me on the phone to welcome me to Morristown. He can tell by my reaction that I am sad leaving St. Agnes Parish.

"Monsignor," I say, "I have plans to visit my family in Ireland for the month of August."

"No problem," he replies. "We will have a bon voyage party here for you and your good friends from St. Agnes before you go."

I learn that he is already of the post-Vatican II mindset. Lay leaders present the first and second readings at Mass. The director of music rehearses the hymns with the congregation, and the choir sings the post-communion hymn in four-part harmony. St. Margaret's is one of the first parishes in the Diocese of Paterson to have altar girls and lay women readers at Sunday liturgies.

I have been in Morristown only four months when Ann Logan, one of the more ecumenical members of St. Margaret's, calls me, saying, "I'm inviting you to come with me to a Christian Dialogue program. You will enjoy it, as you have talked about pursuing Christian Unity in your homilies."

"Sure, Ann, I'll pick you up and you can tell me all about the group while we drive to the meeting."

Following the dictates of Pope John XXIII, two pastoral colleagues— Ambrose Clark, a Benedictine monk, and the Reverend Jim Strange, an American Baptist minister—organize a series of monthly living-room dialogues at different people's homes. All the Christian faiths are represented (i.e., Catholics, both high-and low-church Episcopalians, Lutherans, Methodists, Presbyterians, and both American and AME Zion Baptists). I pick up my new friend, Ann, and we head to my first dialogue with Protestants.

Ambrose and Jim give me, the young priest with the Irish brogue, a warm welcome. My first "living room dialogue" session is fruitful on both a social and spiritual level. I am on my way to becoming a leader of the eternal journey toward Christian Unity. For me personally, Christian Unity is not going to be easy. It will involve a lot of hard work to overcome the childish prejudices I learned from my family and teachers at Legaginney National School in Ireland.

The major hurdle is the naïve view that Irish Catholics are the only ones who will get into heaven. For me, it means rethinking, suspending judgment, and forgiving all the horrible things the British Protestants did to my Irish Catholic forefathers. I pray to Jesus, the ultimate guide and inspiration. I listen to His voice calling me to reconciliation with the separated brethren and asking me to put aside my Irish-Catholic pride and my desire for retaliation. The enthusiasm of Ambrose and Jim is touching my hard heart and pushing me to see and accept my fellow Protestants as equal pilgrims in a broken Church that Vatican Council II is now promising to mend.

CHAPTER III
Vatican Council II: Third Session

The cardinals, bishops and *periti* were greeted with a surprise when they arrived at the Vatican on September 14, 1964, for the Council's third session. Eight religious women in full habit, who represented all the major orders of the Catholic world, and seven laywomen, their heads covered, were seated in the gallery with writing pads and pens, ready to take notes and report back to their communities.

Without the gridlock that so often accompanies some major pieces of federal legislation in Washington, D.C., the Council Fathers worked, studied, argued, discussed, and resolved the problems put before them with amazing speed. In as many months, the Council passed three history-making schemata—*Ecumenism, Eastern Rite Churches, and the Dogmatic Constitution on the Church*—that their various commissions presented to the full Council membership.

To no one's surprise, and to the joy of most progressives and all conservative members of the Council, Pope Paul VI reaffirmed Mary, the mother of Jesus, as the "Mother of the Church." Two months later as he prepared to end the session, he astonished the Catholic world with a headline-grabbing announcement of a change in the required period of fasting before receiving Holy Communion. In keeping with his belief that lay Catholics should receive the body and blood of Christ as often as possible, the millennia-long tradition of overnight fasting was reduced to three hours.

As an ecumenist I was moved when the Council Fathers reminded the entire Christian world that Jesus Christ founded one Church, not hundreds of churches. They reached out to other Christian churches as part of the renewal of Catholicism. Excluding Christian Dialogue would have been interpreted as a fruitless effort at revitalization and have given credence to such protests as "There go the arrogant papists, ignoring us, treating us fellow Christians as second-class citizens."

The primary hope of the Council Fathers was that by mutual prayer, study and dialogue the separated Christian churches would, in time, reunite. This was a change from the dictates of the 1917 Canon, which forbade the Catholic laity and clergy from assisting or participating in any way at non-Catholic religious services. Many Catholics will remember with regret not even being able to "passively participate" at the funerals of their non-Catholic neighbors. There were exceptions to the rule only when the local bishop granted a Catholic person permission to attend a wedding or funeral at a Protestant church, provided there was no danger of scandal.

I attended the wedding of a Catholic and non-Catholic in the non-Catholic bride's church. As the pastor led the congregation in the liturgy, I, dressed in my customary alb and stole, sat in the sanctuary and witnessed the vows of both the bride and groom. Near the end of the liturgy, the pastor got weak. I helped him off the altar to sit in my chair while I went on the altar to finish the service. The pastor recovered by the end of the ceremony, ascended the altar, and proceeded to eulogize my fraternal spirit, saying, "Finbarr is a true brother who came to my rescue today, demonstrating his ecumenical spirit in finishing the liturgy since I was unable to do so."

I replied, "Thank you, Reverend." Meanwhile, I was afraid that one of the conservative Catholics who witnessed my action would call the bishop's office and report, "Our pastor Father Finbarr led the liturgy in a Protestant church today."

In John 13:34, Jesus gives his apostles a new commandment: "That you love one another, even as I have loved you . . ." And shortly before His death, he prays to His Father, speaking the ardent words found in John 17:21: "That they may all be one, as you, Father, are in me, and I in you, that they may also be one in us, so that the world may believe you sent me." Can these two-thousand-year-old words be fulfilled?

The *Pastoral Constitution on the Church in the Modern World, Gaudium et Spes,* one of the most important documents to come from Vatican Council II, was designed by the progressive Council Fathers to guide the Church for several centuries. Unfortunately, the performance of the Catholic Church over the following fifty years tells a different story. In the March 2010 edition of the newsletter *The Word from WEORC* (an Old English word for work), Dermot Keary writes, "As I watched John Paul II, and now Benedict XVI, burying the Council and its decrees, but mostly its spirit, I am close to giving up hope . . ." and, speaking for Vatican II Catholics, he adds, "Mostly, we have all rolled over and played dead while the conservatives continue to pound nails in the lid of the Council's coffin."

Despite what has happened since 1965, it is important to hold to these thoughts from the introductory sections of *The Church in the Modern World*: "Inspired by no earthly ambition, the Church seeks but a solitary goal: to carry forward the work of Christ under the lead of the befriending Spirit. And Christ entered this world to give witness to the truth, to rescue and not to sit in judgment, to serve and not to be served[1] . . . To carry out such a task, the Church has always had the duty of scrutinizing the signs of the times and interpreting them in the light of the Gospel."

In preparing *The Church in the Modern World,* the Council Fathers, perplexed by the cruel treatment people inflict on one another, recognized that the human race had settled into a period of upheaval with far-reaching consequences. The social and cultural changes not only affected mankind's spirituality and practice of its faith, but also presented an old problem in a new and challenging light. The Council Fathers asked themselves some obvious questions: Why is the majority of the world's population still tormented by hunger, poverty and illiteracy despite the advances in psychology, social sciences, biology and agriculture? If humanity progresses scientifically, intellectually and socially, why are the world's goods, knowledge and medicines not more evenly distributed among the vast numbers of the poor and helpless?

While respecting the desire for personal freedom and competition, the Council Fathers addressed the propensity of more powerful nations to dominate the weaker ones by challenging us with the words of the prophet Isaiah: "They will turn their swords into plough-shares, their spears into pruning hooks. One nation shall not lift its sword against another nor shall they train for war" (Isaiah 2:4). Is this just a dream? How long can the world wait for the prophecy of Isaiah to be fulfilled?

* * *

In my ministry as a parish priest, the drama unfolding on the international stage was reflected in our attention to local missionaries and Catholic Charities, who were reaching out to the poor, uneducated and un-churched. The Council Fathers, however, did not limit themselves to such matters, but ventured into the realm of more intimate settings.

"The well-being of the individual person and of Christian society is intimately linked to the healthy condition by Marriage and Family" was a notion included in the *The Church in the Modern World*, and the emphasis placed on it would have extensive and very personal implications for me as I pursued my ministry to engaged couples.

The Council Fathers expected to be allowed to discuss and advise the pope regarding possible revision of the Church's teaching on human reproduction as part of their mission to modernize the Church and to make the living of sacramental marriage more relevant in the modern world. But (ironically, for better or worse) Paul VI took the issue of human reproduction off the agenda and reserved for himself and his commission the right to legislate what happens in the bedroom between a husband and wife.

Pope John XXIII had appointed a commission of six theologians to guide him on this matter. Paul VI took over this advisory board. In keeping with the broader tone of inclusion that he initiated when he took over the Council, he added some lay members, including married couples with expertise from different fields. This commission was given the task of reviewing all previous documents, including encyclicals written by Paul VI's predecessors that condemned artificial birth-control as intrinsically evil.

Those of us in pre-marriage ministry at that time were divided. The majority felt that giving young married couples the freedom to use contraceptives would increase their communication and marital satisfaction, while a minority waited for the pope to tell them what was right and how to communicate the pope's decision to their parishioners.

Paul VI's commission took more than a year to reach a decision. They finished their assignment in 1966 and passed their results to the pope. The report was meant to be held in confidence. That didn't happen. It was leaked to two Catholic newspapers, *The Tablet* in London and the *National Catholic Reporter* in Kansas City. The decision was not unanimous, so confusion followed. The majority of the commission had voted that the Church *should* change its teaching, while a minority argued that the Church *could not* change its teaching since it was a matter of God's law, not man's.

The pope was neither swayed by the arguments of the majority nor by their theological reasoning. He chose instead to support the minority on the commission and his conservative colleagues. Progressive theologians wrote that the pope was heavily influenced by a few conservative cardinals and bishops, while others blamed the *Curia*. His dramatic encyclical, *Humanae Vitae* (Human Life), was released to the world on July 25, 1968.

Not only does the encyclical demand that each and every act of conjugal love between husband and wife be open to the procreation of children, but it predicted dire consequences should contraception and sterilization become more widespread. Some of this was old news. At the close of the nineteenth century, prominent suffragists like Elizabeth Cady Stanton and Susan B. Anthony spoke out to condemn contraception because it was degrading to women and merely an advantage for men, allowing them to act irresponsibly and not be accountable for their actions.[2]

Life, however, has a way of sidestepping the Council Fathers, the *Curia*, the *periti* and the pope. As early as the 1920s, Margaret Sanger, an American nurse, advocated the use of birth control for the physical, mental and emotional well-being of poor women, and, indeed, all women everywhere.[3] She set up a commission of her own to lobby for birth control laws and the establishment of clinics around the world. From the very beginning, *Humanae Vitae* struggled for acceptance because the majority of women of childbearing age were already enlightened about a more practical way of living.

The ongoing battle between conservative Catholics and Vatican II liberals became more obvious and cantankerous as a result of the promulgation of *Humanae Vitae*. Conservatives supported and accepted the encyclical. Progressive theologians, including Father Charles Curran, a professor of theology at the Catholic University in Washington, and Father Bernard Haering, a German theological professor who belonged to the Redemptorist Order, led a worldwide dissent to the encyclical on the basis that the issue of reproduction of the human species is a personal decision that should be left solely to the couples.

CHAPTER IV

Dialogue Bubble in Morristown

While *"Aggiornamento"* became the cry of the Vatican II Fathers adapting the Church's teaching and liturgy to the modern world on the international stage, our local ecumenical Dialogue Committee in Morristown, New Jersey, was busy building bridges of mutual understanding and respect for other Christian denominations. After two years we lost two of our principal leaders. Father Ambrose Clark was promoted to Abbot of the Benedictine Newark's Abbey in New Jersey. The Reverend Jim Strange was called to be pastor of a large Baptist congregation in Tampa, Florida. Two younger clerical "whippersnappers"—Reverend Preston Mears, the twenty-eight-year-old curate at St. Peter's Episcopal Church, and I, the thirty-two-year-old associate pastor of St. Margaret of Scotland Church—became the leaders by default.

We were not alone. Father Bob Harvey, senior assistant at St. Peter's Episcopal, offered his services, saying, "Just in case you two young guys run into trouble with your older bosses, I will be here to bridge the gap." He added with a smile, "My gray hairs will add a sense of maturity to the team."

"Thank you, Bob, your support is deeply appreciated," I replied.

The unbridled enthusiasm we "youngsters" presented to the senior pastors, many of whom were more than twice our age, was received with good-natured indulgence. They got their first shock when Preston and I called an emergency meeting of all the clergy in town with only twenty-four hours notice. The majority of the clergy attended the meeting. But before we had a chance to explain the rationale behind our emergency, the Reverend Hughes Garvin, pastor of St. Peter's, let us know how upset he was. He demanded, "By what authority do two junior clergy have the right to call us all to a meeting and give us only twenty-four hours notice?"

Irish luck was on our side, as the Reverend Henry B. Cannon, known to us as Brev. Cannon, spoke up in our defense by saying, "Wait a minute, Hughes. Let them explain the emergency to us." Then, grinning at his fellow ministers, he added, "Sometimes the Holy Spirit works through young ministers like these better than through old folks like us."

Preston stood up and graciously apologized for any inconvenience that we caused. He thanked Brev. Cannon for his support and said, "I will let Father Finbarr explain what is happening, and why we felt that the situation required your immediate attention."

Standing up, I addressed the group in a contrite tone. "You will remember when we spoke to you at the last monthly Clergy Council Meeting of our plans to hold weekly ecumenical services in each of the churches in town, during the six weeks of Lent?" They all nodded "yes."

I continued. "Well, we ran into a major conflict at my church, St. Margaret's." I explained our dilemma, this time adding an apologetic smile, "Without my knowledge, and despite our plans, my pastor scheduled a parish mission (or retreat) for the first week of Lent. Fortunately, the preacher, a Holy Ghost Father named Father Hanley, stopped by a few days ago to check his schedule and make sure we were prepared to accommodate the large crowd of parishioners that he expected each evening. I told Father Hanley that this parish mission couldn't happen, as we had already scheduled and advertised an ecumenical six-week program for all the churches in Morristown, starting with St. Margaret's during the first week of Lent. Perhaps it was the look on my face that told him this was one Irishman who was not going to give in. He proposed melding both programs for the first week by having pulpit dialogues for the first six evenings, with him in one pulpit representing Roman Catholics and one of you in the second pulpit on the other side of the sanctuary. Each preacher would speak about their own denomination's beliefs and practices. Later, in the school auditorium downstairs, the laity would be able to engage in dialogue with the help of a facilitator."

The silence that followed was awkward, but interesting. Reverend Garvin spoke first, asking a pivotal question. "Finbarr, do you have the approval of your pastor, Monsignor Haag, for this request?"

"Of course, Reverend," I replied.

Later in the rectory when I reported the details and Garvin's question to my boss Monsignor Haag, he teased me, saying, "Thank God and all his holy angels! There is one pastor in Morristown who can control the upstart curates."

Preston and I were relieved and immediately started to promote the Pulpit Dialogues scheduled to begin in one month. We had no trouble getting a representative minister from each of the five denominations to volunteer as a preacher. When we spoke to Father Jack Derricks, pastor of Assumption of the Blessed Virgin Parish, and Reverend Jackson of the Afro-American AME Zion Church, we got nothing but enthusiasm and smiles of approval. They asked, "How can we help?"

Once again I thought of *aggiornamento* as I replied, "You can thank the good Pope John XXIII. He is the one who opened up the doors and windows of the Catholic Church and encouraged this to happen."

With considerable promotion, we stimulated the church members of Morristown with an article in the *Morris County Daily Record* that encouraged Christians from the neighboring towns to come to St. Margaret's on the first Monday of Lent. Father Hanley, a charismatic preacher, addressed a full church and created a non-threatening atmosphere. He introduced Reverend Robert Harvey, from the Episcopal Church, as his co-preacher.

Each evening Father Hanley referred to Vatican Council II, which had completed its fourth and final session only a few months previously. He spoke openly of how both Popes John and Paul wished that we create steps towards Christian Unity. Father Hanley was careful not to refer to the traditional Catholic belief that Catholicism is the one true faith established by Jesus Christ, knowing that this belief was, and still is, offensive to other Christian denominations.

All of the attendees were invited downstairs to enjoy refreshments prepared by the women of the Rosary Society. This welcoming atmosphere helped continue the dialogue on what was shared by both preachers in the sanctuary. The first meeting set the tone for the five meetings to follow, when the evening's focus was shared in turn by the Methodists, Presbyterians, Baptists (both American and Southern Baptists) and AME Zion.

We bid farewell to Father Hanley and thanked him for the pioneering spirit of ecumenism he had created during this first history-making week. Preston and I quietly rejoiced on how the "upstart curates" had inspired the older clergy and how happy we were that over two thousand people participated in the dialogue services during the six days.

Morristown became an ecumenical town. When I walked the streets to shop or mail my letters and someone called out "Hi, Father Finbarr," I didn't know whether I was being addressed by a parishioner or a member of another congregation. Some of our own diocesan priests felt we were moving too quickly and were afraid that the Catholic Church would lose its self-described dominance among other Christian Churches. I didn't share that opinion. I believed that Preston and I were being moved by the call of Jesus: "A new commandment I give you, that you love one another: that as I have loved you; you also must love one another. By this will all men know you are my disciples, if you have love for one another" (John 13:34-35). St. Margaret's was truly becoming a Vatican II community.

A very unusual incident that occurred six months after Father Hanley left was an example of changes that filtered down from the Council to the local parishes. The liturgical restrictions placed on priests by Canon Law forbade them from witnessing the marriage of couples anywhere except in a Catholic church. The only exception was when one party was Jewish: then a priest was allowed to be an official witness with a rabbi in a synagogue or restaurant. The liturgical reform of the Council removed this restriction.

I received a call from an Episcopalian bride wishing to marry a Catholic gentleman in an Episcopal church. Both she and her prospective husband were willing to go through the necessary dispensations for the interfaith marriage and have a Catholic priest witness the marriage for validity. The groom's Catholic pastor refused to help them. Both parties were active members of their churches, and her fiancé was willing to meet the request of the bride and her family to have the ceremony in a church of their faith.

When I asked her why she had come to me, she smiled and admitted, "I went to a few priests and asked them if they would marry us. They were all defensive and gave excuses until we met one priest who said, 'Go see Father Finbarr Corr at St. Margaret's in Morristown, and I bet he will do it.' So, here we are, asking you."

They were very appreciative of the ceremony we celebrated together at St. Peter's Episcopal Church in Morristown. Later I was told that this was the first interfaith marriage witnessed by a Catholic priest in a non-Catholic church in New Jersey. I accepted it as a compliment to our faith community in Morristown and to the foresight of the good Pope John XXIII, who made all these sensitive changes possible.

Unfortunately, I spent only three years in Morristown as an associate pastor. I was blessed with having an open-minded pastor who approved of my progressive ideas to extend our ministry to include other Christian churches in town. We were both excited when I received and accepted an invitation to give three Sunday-night conferences at the Methodist Church on the Green in Morristown. The topic I was to share with a full church was "A Catholic Priest critiques John Wesley." (Wesley was an Anglican theologian who founded the Methodist movement in the early eighteenth century. His brother Charles, also a priest in the Church of England, wrote many of the well-known hymns sung in Protestant churches. Most Christians are familiar with "Hark the Herald Angels Sing," one of his best-loved Christmas hymns.)

During my three years at St. Margaret's, I went back to college and earned a Master's Degree in Pastoral Counseling, which led to my appointment as assistant director of the Diocesan Family Life Bureau. In due time, the bishop appointed me the first full-time director of this very important agency. I was humbled by the bishop's trust in allowing me to become a pioneer in establishing Family Life programs in all one hundred parishes of the diocese.

Before I move back to Paterson, I witnessed the beginning of a dialogue between a few couples from St. Margaret's Parish and our Jewish neighbors, who worshiped in the synagogue across the street. This time I was not the initiator or leader. My life-long ecumenical friends, Ann Logan and her husband Ralph, had already befriended several couples from the synagogue. The rabbi and I sat in on their discussions—not as moderators, but simply as resources to help with discussions on the Messiah for whom the Jews wait and on Jesus Christ, whom we celebrate as our Lord and Savior. The discussions included both our understanding of God as Creator, the role of Moses and all the prophets, and, lastly, our belief in angels. The rabbi became comfortable enough to participate in the annual Thanksgiving ecumenical service at St. Margaret's, and usually invited two or three couples from his synagogue to join him.

*   *   *

This is not the end of the story. There was a little irony, which will be recorded here. Twenty years later I resigned the priesthood to marry. We bought a house and moved to Convent Station, a suburb of Morristown. I walked out one morning to introduce myself to our new neighbors, Phil and Adele Greenberg. While I was chatting with them, Adele gave me a big smile of recognition as she asked, "Aren't you the same Father Finbarr we met years ago when we had the meetings with Catholics at our synagogue in Morristown?" Once again I said to myself, "Thanks to you, Pope John, for opening up another window."

CHAPTER V

New Definition of the Catholic Church

The third session of the Council could be defined as both a "bang" and a "bomb" event. The Council Fathers were ready when Pope Paul VI initiated the third session on September 14, 1964. Pope Paul confirmed the mindset of his predecessor, Pope John XXIII, when he addressed the attendees and told them how the pastoral nature of the Church was about to be renewed. The Council Fathers approved with a "bang" three important schemata that they had been revising since the second session ended on December 4, 1963: *Unitatis Redintegratio*, on ecumenism; *Orientalium Ecclesiarum*, the official view on Protestantism and Eastern Rite Churches; and the *Dogmatic Constitution on the Church, Lumen Gentium*. All were promulgated by Pope Paul VI.

As recorded in Chapter II, the surprise of the third session was Pope Paul's refusal to accept the schema on the sacrament of marriage submitted by the Council Fathers. Conservatives in the Church claimed that Pope Paul showed his conservative theological side when he instructed the bishops to defer the topic of contraception within marriage to him. As a result, many active Catholics lost faith in the Church when he ignored the majority opinion of his appointed commission and promulgated his version of *Humanae Vitae*.

According to Janet Smith, "*Humanae Vitae* predicts a general lowering of morality should contraception become widely available. Women are more open to exploitation by men. There is little need here to demonstrate the consequences of the sexual revolution, for who is not familiar with epidemic teenage pregnancies, venereal diseases, divorces, AIDS, etc.?"[1]

The tension between the conservatives and the progressives seemed to be less obvious during this third session. This may have been because a younger pope, Paul VI, took a more hands-on approach to the Council's deliberations than did the aging and sickly Pope John XXIII.

The document of vital importance to the progressives was *Lumen Gentium* (Latin: Light of Nations). It was promulgated by Pope Paul VI on November 21, 1964, following a positive vote of 2,151 to 5. The surprise for progressive Catholics was the declaration in the second chapter of *Lumen Gentium* that the Church is "the People of God." Progressives believed that this document would put an end to Catholics thinking of the Church as the pope and hierarchy. This new definition influenced the worldview of Catholicism in the 1960s and is now being used by priest reform groups like the Association of Irish Catholic Priests.

Lumen Gentium clarified how this happened: "Christ instituted the new covenant—that is to say, the new testament in His blood—by calling together a people made up of Jews and Gentiles, making them one, not according to the flesh but in the spirit" (*LG* 2). The role of the bishops is redefined as a *college*: "The order of bishops is the successor to the college of the apostles in teaching authority and pastoral rule. Thus the apostolic body continues without a break. . . . The episcopal order is the subject of supreme and full power over the universal church, provided that we understand this power can be exercised only with the consent of the Roman Pontiff" *(LG* 3).

I doubt that any objective Catholic who follows the activities of the bishops, either here in the United States or worldwide, can recall the College of Bishops acting with supreme and full power over the universal church. One of my progressive Catholic colleagues recently stated, "The role and power of the College of Bishops is, regretfully, being chipped away by the powerful *Curia* in Rome."

Conservative bishops at the Council objected to the proposed description of the bishops of the Catholic Church as a college with supreme power. They thought that this proposal, which had a scriptural backing, would minimize the power of the pope. However, the vote that followed passed with a resounding majority. The conservative minority didn't give up. They proposed forty-seven amendments to Chapter 3 of *Lumen Gentium*.

Pope Paul VI opened the fourth and final session of the Council on September 14, 1965, by establishing the Synod of Bishops. This permanent structure was supposed to preserve close cooperation of the bishops of the world and the Roman Pontiff after the Council concluded. Church historians report that this cooperation lasted for a relatively short time. Conservatives said that this doctrine of double supreme authority (Canon 336) of bishops and pope was contrary to the teaching contained in the First Vatican Council and Pope Leo's encyclical *Satis Cognitum*, which emphasized the primacy of the pope.

One of the more controversial schemas passed at the Council and promulgated by Pope Paul VI on November 21, 1964, was the *Decree for the Catholic Churches of the Eastern Rite, Orientalium Ecclesiarum*. The Council Fathers recognized the validity of the sacred orders of bishops and priests in the Eastern Orthodox Churches, even if outside the jurisdiction of the Roman Pontiff. Furthermore, the Council Fathers reminded the Eastern Churches of their shared responsibility, with the Apostolic See of Rome, to promote the unity of all Christian Churches, especially Eastern Christians, by prayer and by collaboration.

Paragraph 25 of the same schema has caused a serious split between progressive and conservative theologians. Progressive theologians claim that this paragraph approves of Eastern Christians receiving the Eucharist in a Latin Rite church, provided they profess their faith in the Holy Catholic Church and are disposed to receiving the body and blood of Christ.

Several conservative theologians make a totally opposite interpretation, saying that, since all non-Catholics are excluded from salvation, they are automatically forbidden from receiving Holy Communion in a Latin Rite Church. Other theologians argue that it is not possible for the categories of modern thinking to be applied to Catholic doctrine because the doctrines of the Catholic Church are immutable and therefore cannot be reconciled with present-day advances. A few conservative theologians have gone so far as to accuse Popes John

XXIII and Paul VI of heresy, stating that the two popes approved of modernist teachings previously condemned by their predecessors—Pope Pius X in his 1907 decree *Lamentabili* and Pope Pius XII in his 1950 encyclical *Humani Generis.*

The ongoing conflict between conservative theologians and modern progressive theologians is as old as the Church itself. An example in current headlines in the public and Catholic press is the uproar of conservative Catholics against Pope Benedict XVI's reply to a question by Peter Seewald, a German journalist, in an interview included in Seewald's book *Light of the World.*[2] The pope stated that the use of condoms could be justified in some cases—for example, preventing AIDS. Because they feared that the statement would lead the Church into error, the conservatives jumped all over Benedict, accusing him of giving concessions to secularists in the Church.

Pope Benedict didn't change any doctrine. He invoked the principle of "lesser evil," meaning that a man with AIDS could choose the lesser evil of using a condom rather than passing on the horrible disease of AIDS to his partner. According to *New York Times* reporter David Gibson, "Father Timothy Finigan, a Catholic priest from Britain, wrote in his blog, 'I'm sorry. I love the Holy Father very much; he is a deeply holy man and has done a great deal for the Church. On this particular issue I disagree with him.' Another conservative Catholic blogger posted the title of Seewald's book above a picture of Pandora opening a box and releasing all of the world's evils."[3]

Lest we be accused of picking on the Catholic Church as the only organization that suffers from conservative and progressive conflict, there is an analogous situation in America's highly respected judicial system. Supreme Court Justices Scalia and Thomas insist on interpreting the United States Constitution with a more conservative and literal intent based on its context in 1776. In contrast, their fellow justices interpret the Constitution as seems applicable in today's society. Common sense tells us that both the Catholic Church and U.S. laws must adapt to the world of the twenty-first century.

CHAPTER VI
Ireland before Vatican II

For all of us, life is a journey, and for each of us it begins at a time and place that leaves an indelible mark on our spiritual and psychological well-being. My personal journey began in Legaginney, County Cavan, Ireland, in the mid-1930s. I was one of nine children in a typical large, Irish-Catholic family. I was expected to begin my day kneeling by my bedside as I recited my morning prayers. If I was outside playing in the evening or visiting my schoolmates, I was obliged to be home in time for the family rosary.

Prior to Vatican Council II, being Catholic and being Irish were one and the same. In 1945 if anybody asked me, "Who are you anyway, Finbarr Corr?" my answer was, "I am Catholic, I serve as an altar boy at Sunday Mass." Serving Sunday Mass was the highlight of my week.

Similarly, if I was asked who the most important people in the parish were, I did not list the local grocery store owner or a big farmer. I replied without hesitation, "Our parish pastor, Father McGauran, and Master McCarthy, the principal of our local grammar school."

We continued to hold the parish priest and, in fact, all Catholic priests in reverential awe during the 1940s and 1950s. They not only forgave our sins in the confessional, but they also told us how to behave as they preached each Sunday from the altar. For all practical purposes the laity treated them as if they were infallible. Frequently you would hear a parishioner say, "I tell you it is the truth. Didn't Father McGauran say so from the altar a few Sundays ago?"

During this period, Catholic adults and children were expected to attend a full Mass on Sundays and holy days of obligation. And 99 percent of them did. The only exception I remember was an uncle in our family, related through marriage. In a way, his behavior was prophetic of the thinking today of many of adult Catholics in Ireland, who see themselves as liberated from the tyrannical control of the Catholic Church. Uncle Jim just went to church for weddings and funerals.

Conversely, being Catholic during this period meant you simply believed what the priest told you, and you did what he told you to do. The only time I was excused from Sunday Mass attendance was when I was sick. If I missed Mass because of illness, my mother didn't allow me to go out and play with friends or attend any local football game for the rest of the day. If I was too sick to attend Mass, it followed that I was too sick for any other activity. The reality was that I was one of the millions of Catholics born in "a backward land dominated and shaped by the Roman Church."[1]

There is no comparison between the seeming clarity and simplicity of the pre-Vatican II Irish Church and the confusion experienced in the Church of today's Irish Catholics. The four pillars were clear and concise:

1. Devotion to the Blessed Trinity of the Father, Son and Holy Ghost (later renamed the Holy Spirit). This belief was so strong that, after the successful 1916 rebellion, Eamon De Valera, the political leader in Ireland, "drafted a constitution side by side with the powerful archbishop of Dublin, John Charles McQuaid, which gave the Catholic Church a special role in state affairs and which to this day begins with the words 'In the name of the Most Holy Trinity.'"[2]

2. Devotion to the Virgin Mary, the mother of our Savior Jesus Christ. Ireland is the only country in the world, to my knowledge, that has a special name for the mother of God in its native Gaelic language (i.e., Muire). The custom continues to this day

in Ireland that Catholic parents, out of respect for Mary's special role, never christen their daughters Muire.

3. Devotion to the celebration of the Holy Mass, which commemorates the Last Supper when Jesus gave us the institution of transubstantiating bread and wine into His own body and blood. Through dungeon, fire and sword, the priests of Ireland celebrated Mass for the faithful.

4. Unwavering loyalty to his Holy Father the Pope in all circumstances.

In 1965 when Pope Paul VI expanded the commission of theologians and married couples to research the morality of using artificial contraception, many progressive priests hoped that Pope Paul would leave it up to the consciences of couples to regulate conception. It was quickly rumored that this was going to be the recommendation of the committee to the Holy Father.

I was in Ireland on July 25, 1968, when disappointing news made headlines in the Irish newspapers: POPE PAUL VI FORBIDS CATHOLIC COUPLES USING ARTIFICIAL MEANS TO REGULATE CONCEPTION. The related decree *Humanae Vitae*, subtitled *The Regulation of Birth*, greatly depressed many devout Catholics.

That moment is still crystal clear in my mind. I tried to hide my feelings from my ailing mother in the hospital, but I couldn't fool her. She said with a smile, "Finbarr, you don't seem to be yourself today. What's wrong?" I didn't lie to my mother; I told her why I was sad. She replied as the average pre-Vatican II Irish Catholic would have, saying, "If the pope has spoken, that settles the issue for everybody." I didn't argue the point with my mom.

As I left the hospital, I thought that this is the Church I have loved and will always love in spite of moments like this. I reminded myself how much I had grown educationally, spiritually and emotionally through it, but then again I felt free to critique its teaching and the behavior of its hierarchy and clergy. None of them are perfect or sinless, just as I am not perfect or sinless.

Looking back at my days as a boarder at St. Patrick's College, Cavan, where I attended high school, I now know that I was a very naïve young man. Just fourteen years old, I was still in awe of priests, who were then my teachers and spiritual directors. I also felt obliged to respect the students who were my seniors. I was not prepared emotionally for what I would experience during the next five years.

It was customary during this time in Ireland to educate children in the fundamentals of human sexuality. I also learned the basics of male and female sexual intercourse from my classmates in grammar school. I witnessed my oldest brother necking and petting with his girlfriend along the railroad tracks near our home in Legaginney.

After several months at St. Patrick's, an all-boys boarding school, I learned that senior boys, in the absence of girls, would satisfy their desires by approaching younger boys in their beds at night for sexual favors. I noticed that the younger boys chosen had effeminate characteristics that I, fortunately, lacked. The behavior was called *mugging*. Although condemned as sinful by the visiting priest of the Redemptorist Order as he conducted the annual retreat for the student body, it continued

Reverend Patrick Hederman, abbot of the Glendstal Abbey in Limerick, described the church of this period as "a concentration camp where the hierarchy controlled everybody and everything. They told you that if you masturbated it meant you were impure and had allowed the devil to work on you."[3]

It is no wonder that thousands of young boys developed guilt complexes that lingered into their senior years. To add to the confusion I felt as a young teenager at St. Patrick's, a few of the priest teachers administered cruel punishment.

One language teacher actually came to class with a large cane hidden beneath his black cassock. I can still see him entering our classroom on a Monday morning, angry because his favorite football team was beaten the day before. "Mr. Corr, decline for me if you can such and such a verb." If I failed to decline it perfectly, he pulled out the cane and gave me three strikes on each hand, leaving welts, and said, "This will remind you to study your Latin tonight."

Another priest teacher, who will also remain nameless, administered similar punishment for homework not completed to his satisfaction. When I got a little older, I learned that this cruel priest was also an active pedophile. He invited effeminate freshmen and sophomores to his room after study hall on Sunday evenings, supposedly to listen to the Top Ten tunes on Radio Eireann. At the end of the evening he would invite one young boy to stay behind to brush his cassock. He then sexually molested the student before he allowed the boy to rejoin his sleeping classmates in the dormitory.

I knew it was wrong, but neither my classmates nor I felt that it was something we should report to the bishop or civil authorities. I do recall hearing that four of five of the senior boys felt differently. They went as a group to the bishop, who lived near St. Patrick's, and demanded that the bishop remove this priest and his priest colleague, who had the same propensity for abusing boys at the college. Before we returned to college the following September, one priest was transferred to the Diocese of Grand Rapids, Michigan, the second to a diocese in England.

I was fortunate that the positive influence of my parents and a strong Christian faith, nourished at my own home parish of St. Michael's Potahee, kept me well-grounded and didn't distract me from my goal of attending the seminary to be ordained a priest. I followed the pre-Vatican II rituals and served Mass in Latin, said a daily rosary in honor of our Blessed Lady, and on four occasions participated in what is commonly called in Ireland "the toughest pilgrimage in the world." The three-day pilgrimage ritual, an almost continuous cycle of prayer and liturgies, is on St. Patrick's Purgatory, an island in the center of Lough Derg, in County Donegal, where tradition tells us that Patrick spent many days of praying and fasting while he established the Catholic Church in Ireland (AD 432-461).

Socially, I did all the normal things typical of a teenager in Ireland during this period. I played Gaelic football, went to parish dances, and dated girls. I was always careful not to tell the girls or my male friends that I might enter the priesthood.

Looking back at that time, I recall never doubting that I could live a celibate life. I didn't see any contradiction between young men with strong sexual desires and entering the celibate priesthood. I ask myself today whether I was too naïve, believing that the grace of the sacrament of holy orders would be strong enough to keep me celibate for fifty years. Or was I actually unconsciously wishing that the Catholic Church would finally see that mandatory celibacy is unrealistic and irrational for sexually healthy males?

The pre-Vatican II Church did not resolve the issue. Only time will tell whether the Church of the post-Vatican II era, which now ordains married deacons, will take the next step and elevate these married deacons to the priesthood.

CHAPTER VII
Child Abuse in Irish Institutions

While pedophile priests were sexually abusing young boys at St. Patrick's College, Cavan, and senior boys were meeting their sexual desires by mugging sophomore and freshmen boys after lights out in the dormitories and bedrooms, a much greater tragedy was afflicting children in the residential institutions managed by Catholic religious congregations in Ireland. More than thirty thousand children deemed to be petty thieves, truants or from dysfunctional families were sent to these institutions from the 1930s until the last facilities were closed in the 1990s.

In 2009 the Ryan Report, a nine-year study ordered by the Irish government, finally documented the shameful and disgusting treatment of boys and girls who resided in these institutions during the years from 1936 onward. The report's word to describe the particular degree of sexual molestation of boys in the church-run industrial schools and orphanages was "endemic."[1]

The Irish Christian Brothers in charge of the Artane Industrial School in Dublin were in the eye of the abuse storm from the very beginning. The Brothers administered beatings for infractions as minor as not knowing the Gaelic translation of a word or an addition in arithmetic. At times the beatings were so bruising that the victim sought relief in the infirmary. To escape beatings, savvy boys joined the distinguished Artane Boys Band. The Brothers would never want a boy with a black eye or marks on his face marching with the band in prestigious Croke Park, the national stadium.

A second abusive congregation was the Sisters of Mercy, whose several industrial schools throughout Ireland included the notorious Goldenbridge (officially, St. Vincent's Industrial School, Goldenbridge). According to the Ryan Report, up to the 1970s "the girls [at Goldenbridge] received punishment that was pervasive, unpredictable and arbitrary and used for small infringements . . . [such as] bedwetting" (II: 7.132-140). When exposed by the Ryan Report, the Sisters pledged to donate 128 million euros to compensate the victims. The Irish government replied that the amount was not sufficient.

The Taoiseach (Prime Minister) of Ireland, Bertie Ahern, was the first Irish leader in either the State or the Catholic Church to discuss this tragedy on a national level. Addressing the Irish Parliament on May 5, 1999, he first apologized to the young institutional abuse victims. He asked the victims for forgiveness, saying, "On behalf of the State and all the citizens of the State, the government wishes to make a sincere and long overdue apology to the victims of childhood abuse for our collective failure to intervene, to detect their pain, to come to their rescue." As a follow-up, Taoiseach Ahern and the Irish government commissioned the aforementioned Ryan Report.

When I first read the report in late 2009, I asked myself, "Did the Christian Brothers at the Artane Boys School feel free to abuse boys committed to their school because the boys had committed frivolous crimes or because the boys were orphans?" Four of my classmates at St. Patrick's were also taught by the Christian Brothers, but at a day school in Cavan town. However, none of them ever complained of physical punishment at the hands of the Brothers. This does not change the confidential comment by a resigned Christian Brother that young people living in the two hundred industrial schools run by religious congregations lived in a "climate of fear" where they suffered physical, emotional and sexual abuse (I: 14.01-27).

The fact remains that the government officials who inspected these industrial schools over a period of sixty years failed to stop the beatings and rapes of these unfortunate young inmates. Neither did the Catholic Church authorities, according to the Ryan Report. Individuals who later served as priests in the Vatican II era cannot fail to note the similar mindsets. In both periods Church authorities failed to stop extreme cruelty and sexual abuse of children and tolerated the secrecy imposed by bishops to shelter pedophile priests in their own dioceses.

The Ryan Report revealed that the sexual abuse of children was "managed" with a view towards minimizing the risk of public disclosure and consequent damage to the institution of the Church and the religious congregation. Putting it in layman's terms, the clergy protected the good names of the Catholic Church, the bishops and priests, and to hell with worrying about the poor and the orphaned inmates. The national report described the latter's suffering as "being flogged, kicked and otherwise physically assaulted, scalded, burned and held under water" (III: 7, 9, 13-18).

Why didn't the Department of Education staff, who were (and still are) ultimately charged with the care of children, challenge the congregations to openness and insist upon discipline for the offending priests, brothers and nuns? The report stated that the sexual abuse of children was made known to the staff of the Department of Education, as well as to the police and other bodies.

Was the challenge of prosecuting clergy and nuns at this period of the Catholic ethos in Ireland too difficult for the civil authorities? In the pre-Vatican II Church the answer seemed to be "YES." The report concluded that, although "sexual abuse was known to be a pervasive problem in male religious organizations," each instance "was treated in isolation and secrecy by the authorities and there was no attempt to address the underlying systemic nature of the problem" (Conclusions: 23). In Chapter XXV we will deal with the recidivism of the abuse and the failure of the State and the Church to see pedophilia as an addiction or a psychosexual fixation at a relatively young age.

The Murphy Report, a devastating critique of the Archdiocese of Dublin, was also released in 2009. Prior to its release, Dublin's Archbishop Diarmuid Martin used his Holy Thursday homily to prepare the laity for news that would shake the very foundation of the archdiocese. He warned, "It will shock all of us and will make each of us and the entire church in Dublin a humbler church."[2]

The Murphy Report stated: "The Dublin archdiocese's preoccupations in dealing with child sex abuse, at least until the mid-1990s, were secrecy, avoidance of scandal, protection of the reputation of the Church, and the preservation of its assets. All other considerations including the welfare of children and justice for victims were subordinated to these priorities. Any applicable guidelines from the Vatican were minimal and inadequate. The archdiocese did not implement its own Canon Law and also did its best to avoid any application of the law of the State."[3]

Church authorities all over Ireland and for most of the Catholic world were slow to take a public stance in condemning the crimes of pedophile priests and the sexual and physical abuse of children. Looking back, it is easy to see that the civil authorities in Ireland gave preferential treatment to bishops during this pre-Vatican II period. To add to the scandal surrounding the Irish bishops and the Department of Education, a document was disclosed on Radio Television Eire on January 17, 2011.

This confidential document, *Crimen Sollicitationis*, was a response from the apostolic nuncio to Ireland, Archbishop Luciano Storero, to the bishops of Ireland on the sexual abuse of minors by clerics. (See Appendix.) It stated that the *Congregation for the Clergy* wished to emphasize the need to conform to Canonical norms of the Church, while it hesitated to demand "Mandatory Reporting" to civil authorities. In layman's terms, it was a sin for a cleric to sexually abuse a child, but there was no mention that it was a crime punishable by civil authorities and should be reported.[4]

This document, written by Storero on January 31, 1997, and marked Strictly Confidential, clearly contradicted the Vatican's claim that the Church leaders in Rome never sought control of abuse cases and that the official Roman Catholic Church did not impede criminal investigations of child abuse suspects. Colm O'Gorman, an outspoken victim of abuse in Ireland and now the director of Amnesty International in Ireland says, "The Vatican was at the root of the problem. Any suggestion that they have not deliberately and willfully been instructing bishops not to report [pedophile] priests to appropriate civil authorities is now proven to be ridiculous."[5]

In 2006 O'Gorman filmed *Sex Crimes and the Vatican* for the BBC. The documentary claimed that Cardinal Joseph Ratzinger enforced *Crimen Sollicitationis* for twenty years before he became Pope Benedict XVI.[6] The abuse victims in Ireland called *Crimen Sollicitationis* a "smoking gun" and said they would use it in lawsuits against the Vatican.

CHAPTER VIII
Father Marcial Maciel Degollado

The young seminarian riding across from me on the train to Fatima in June 1986 immediately caught my attention. It was a very warm evening, and yet he was dressed in a long black cassock and a Roman collar. Large rosary beads hung from his neck. I was dressed in casual and cooler civilian clothes, the customary garb of a priest on vacation. The friendly young man was happy to tell me all about his order, the Legion of Christ. I knew almost nothing about the Legion except that it was a very special favorite of Pope John Paul's. When I asked the seminarian why he chose to wear such a long cassock and Roman collar on such a warm summer evening, he replied quite righteously, "Father Marcial, our founder, decreed that we always wear clerical dress, and we take an oath of loyalty not to question his judgments or decisions."

Father Marcial Maciel Degollado was a powerful, theologically conservative priest born in Mexico in 1920. A charismatic figure with a magnetic personality, Degollado was possibly the best priest-fundraiser in the history of the Catholic Church. At its prime, the conservative order he founded in Mexico in 1941 boasted of having 480 priests serving in twenty countries on five continents, as well as 25,000 seminarians preparing spiritually and educationally to be ordained priests of the order. Degollado's greatest source of pride was his loyalty to the pope and his acceptance by the Vatican *Curia*.

Father Degollado died in 2008. On April 20, 2010, Ross Douthat, a respected journalist from the *New York Times*, wrote, "The last pope [John Paul II] loved him [Father Maciel] and defended him. But we know now that he was a sexually voracious sociopath. And, thanks to a recent exposé by the *National Catholic Reporter*'s Jason Berry, we know the secret of Maciel's Vatican success: he was an extraordinary fundraiser, and those funds often flowed to members of John Paul's inner circle."[1]

The story is shocking. This eighty-one-year-old priest, "leader of the Legion of Christ, a wealthy religious order known for its theological conservatism and loyalty to the pope, was being accused by nine former priests of sexually abusing them years ago as young seminarians."[2] The story is almost too atrocious to be credible. Even if unsubstantiated, it leaves me confused. Two questions keep surfacing in my mind: (1) How could such a creative, ostensibly pious priest be so perverse? and (2) How could an intelligent man like Pope John Paul II be so easily betrayed by this corrupt con man?

I am forced to return to the beginning of Maciel's sordid history. Jason Berry, writing in the *National Catholic Reporter*, relates that "Maciel was expelled from two seminaries for what official history describes as misunderstandings about his desire to start a religious order." He then took a very unusual route to the priesthood. "One of Maciel's uncles, Bishop Francesco Gonzalez Arias of Cuernavaca, Mexico, oversaw his theological training and ordained him a priest in 1944."[3]

The chronology of Maciel's life and ministry is confusing. While the date of his ordination to the priesthood is listed as November 26, 1944, he is credited with founding the Legion of Christ on January 24, 1941, three years earlier. Jason Berry's *National Catholic Reporter* article raised further suspicions about Maciel's sexual maturity. The stories about the Legion's founder go back several years to January 3, 1941, when Maciel gathered thirteen young boys around him to teach them theology.[4] History also records that he laid the groundwork for forming the Legion's lay arm, Regnum Christi, in 1959. Knowing his later behavior, one wonders about his real motivation in enlisting those young boys. With what therapists know about pedophilia, if Maciel were an aspiring candidate for priesthood today, it is doubtful that he would be ordained, even by his uncle bishop. If Father Maciel were my client, I would ask, "Tell me, Father, were you ever molested as a young boy?"

It is coincidental that John Paul II issued an apology for all the sexual abuse committed by pedophile priests in the same week of 2001 that the hideous story of Father Marcial Maciel Degollado's sexual abuse charges hit the Catholic press in the United States. Ross Douthat of the *New York Times* noted the similarity in how the Catholic Church mishandled the priest pedophile crisis worldwide and how for several years the Vatican blocked allegations by the nine men who claimed that Father Maciel had molested them when they were young seminarians.[5]

To many, the case against Maciel is important because it tests the Vatican's resolve to pursue charges related to sexual misconduct at the highest level of the Church. The story of the accuser's case, brought before the *Congregation for the Doctrine of the Faith,* opens a rare lens on the Vatican bureaucracy's response to a delicate case involving a priest who enjoyed Vatican favor. The accusers, seven Mexicans and two Spaniards, tried for many years to reach John Paul II with information about Maciel. Letters from two of the men, sent by diplomatic pouch to John Paul II in 1978 and in 1989, brought no reply.[6]

One story of those nine priests is particularly devastating because of the age at which the victim was recruited. Juan Vaca was invited into the Legion by Maciel when he was only ten years old. Two years later Maciel accompanied this young boy from Mexico to a Legion seminary in Santander, Spain. According to Vaca, Maciel began abusing him at that time, "beginning a psychosexual relationship that he contends he endured for years into adulthood."

"It didn't feel right," Vaca said. "I wanted to go to confession. He told me there was nothing wrong. You don't have to go to confession." Vaca said he pressed Maciel again about his feelings of guilt, only to have Maciel make a Sign of the Cross and say, "Here, I will give you absolution."[7]

In 1976 Father Vaca quit the Legion and joined the diocesan clergy in Rockville Centre Diocese New York. Two years later he showed his new boss, Bishop McGann, an explosive twelve-page letter he had written to Maciel in 1976 to explain why he (Vaca) was quitting the

Legion. Officials of the Rockville Centre Diocese sent Vaca's letter to the pope through the Vatican embassy. They also included a second letter from Father Felix Alcaron, a native of Spain, who resigned the Legion and also joined the Rockville Centre Diocese. The diocese received an acknowledgement for the letters. However, Vaca and Alarcon say they were never contacted by the Vatican.

According to Ross Douthat, "funds from Maciel that flowed to members of John Paul's inner circle" were the primary reason that these accusing letters were blocked and ignored by the Vatican. This inner circle group included Archbishop Stanislaw Dziwisz, the papal secretary, who now serves as Cardinal Dziwisz, the head of the Catholic Church in Poland. Douthat further commented, "Only one churchman comes out . . . looking good. Joseph Ratzinger lectured to a group of Legion priests and was subsequently handed an envelope of money for his charitable use." The cardinal "was tough as nails in a very cordial way, a witness said, and turned the money down."[8]

Pope John II is deceased and thus is unable to correct the mistakes that he and his associates made in overlooking Maciel's crimes. It is left to Pope Benedict XVI to clean house and straighten out the Legion of Christ and Regnum Christi. As he executes both of these functions and apologizes to the world for the crimes of all pedophile priests, Benedict XVI deserves to be remembered as the better pope.

CHAPTER IX

Archbishop John Charles McQuaid and his Successors

Why was the Irish hierarchy from 1962 to 2004 reluctant to accept the *Documents of Vatican Council II*, which would have made the Irish Church more vibrant? The following stories might help answer this question. One story is personal. The other describes the life and ministry of John Charles McQuaid, who from 1940 to 1972 was Archbishop of Dublin, the most powerful Church post in Ireland. His secretive style was echoed by his three successors and was unlike the more open mentality of the current archbishop, Diarmuid Martin.

Archbishop McQuaid and I were both born in County Cavan, although he arrived there in 1895, forty years sooner than I. We attended the same boarding school, St. Patrick's College, Cavan, where we studied Latin and Greek. We also shared June ordinations to the priesthood, although his predated mine by thirty-six years. Our reactions to Vatican II were strikingly different, reflecting the changes brought about by this Council.

Vatican Council II energized and transformed me. I spent from 1969 to 1979 as a Family Life educator and therapist, serving as director of the Diocesan Family Life Bureau in Paterson, New Jersey. I then became pastor of a large congregation in Madison, New Jersey. My work with the fifteen hundred volunteers in the Family Life Bureau prepared me well to lead a post-Vatican II parish.

During those ten years I changed from a "know-it-all" priest to one who was an enabler and facilitator. When I became pastor, many parishioners in Madison already knew as much as, or more than, I about running parish organizations and fundraising. Two volunteer trustees supervised all financial transactions. Two business executives with public relations expertise created a stewardship program that increased the number of volunteers in the parish from one hundred fifty to fifteen hundred and helped boost weekly collections from $4,500 to over $14,000. All of this volunteer activity freed me and two associate pastors to do what we were ordained to do—serve the spiritual needs of the eighteen hundred families in the parish.

As you read about the lives and ministry of McQuaid and the three archbishops who succeeded him in the Dublin archdiocese during the post-Vatican II period, you will learn how they chose to continue the arrogant and secretive leadership that helped create the crisis in the church in Dublin and in all of the Irish Church today. Let's look first at his successors.

Following McQuaid's tenure (1940-1971), the Vatican's *Congregation for Bishops* chose Dermot Ryan, an academic, rather than a pastoral-oriented priest. Surprisingly, McQuaid had fired Ryan when he was teaching liberation theology at the seminary in Dublin. Ryan was named in the Irish government's 2009 Murphy Report for protecting pedophile priests and failing to report some pedophile priests to the Dublin police. According to the report, he joined those "church authorities who were more concerned about the scandals that would be created if they revealed the names of the abusing priests rather than concern for the abused children." He died suddenly in Rome in 1984 of a heart attack. To show their disgust that he was designated as a protector of pedophile priests in the Murphy Report, the Dublin city council changed the name of a Dublin park that had previously been named to honor him.

In the minds of many educated Catholics in Dublin, the *Congregation for Bishops* in Rome compounded its errors when they chose yet another senior academic to succeed Ryan. At that time, Archbishop Kevin McNamara was reportedly one of the two most outspoken conservative members of the Irish hierarchy. Rather than implement the decrees of Vatican Council II, McNamara focused primarily on abortion and divorce issues. His reign was cut short when he died of cancer three years after his coronation as archbishop. In the annals of Catholic Ireland, he was far out of step with his noted contemporary, the more diplomatic Archbishop of Armagh Cardinal Tomas O'Fiaich.

The *Congregation for Bishops* continued to ignore the edicts of Vatican Council II after McNamara's death when, for no pastoral reason, they chose Desmond Connell, a metaphysics professor from University College, Dublin, as the new archbishop. The only apparent reason for Connell's selection was that he was a good friend of Pope Benedict XVI.

In its November 23, 2009, edition, the *Irish Independent* newspaper described Cardinal Connell as a "hugely unpopular Archbishop of Dublin, [whose first major error was] providing a glowing job reference to an American diocese on behalf of one priest abuser."[1] My question is, "Why was the freedom and religious liberty embraced by Vatican Council II interpreted by these leaders as a threat to church order and authority in Ireland. Was their resistance due to a childhood trauma or to some other influence?"

I was fortunate to have a simple but nurturing childhood, typical of Irish-born children. Dad was a hard-working farmer with limited financial resources to feed and educate nine children. Mom was a college graduate whose teaching career was limited to educating her nine children to have a great thirst for knowledge, a desire to fulfill their mission of loving God, and a prayerful relationship with his son Jesus Christ and his Blessed Mother.

John Charles McQuaid was not as lucky as a child. He was born in Cootehill, County Cavan. His father Eugene was a medical doctor who served the local population. There wasn't much money in the house, but "being a doctor's son in Cootehill set him in a patrician mould."[2] His mother Jennie Curry died one week after his birth, and his father signed her death certificate. McQuaid's father remarried a woman named Agnes, who raised John Charles and his sister Helen as if they were her own.

Dr. McQuaid did not tell his children John Charles and Helen that Agnes was not their natural mother. John Charles discovered it only years later from a fellow student at Clongowes Wood Jesuit College. His biographer wrote, "The news seems to have affected him powerfully. When his father died, John Charles had him buried with his mother, not his stepmother. He remains devoted to his stepmother and her children throughout his life."[3]

Believing that the standard of education was not challenging enough at St. Patrick's, John Charles's father transferred him to the renowned Blackrock College in Dublin. It was a perfect decision, as his son's grades improved dramatically. He placed eighth among all of Ireland's classics students, with a first place score of 98 percent in Latin, 96 in Greek and 80 in French. He continued his brilliant scholastic career at University College Dublin. Rather than pursue a career in medicine, as his friends and family expected, he entered the Holy Ghost Novitiate and was ordained a priest on June 29, 1924.

Students of history who enjoy dissecting Vatican Council II's effect on the Catholic world are fascinated by the effects of family background on priests and bishops like McQuaid. In contrast to McQuaid, Angelo Roncalli, Pope John XXIII, was raised in relative poverty. He walked barefoot to school five miles each way and eventually became what all of his family and friends in the Diocese of Bergamo expected, the true servant pope that priests with a post-Vatican II mindset want to emulate.

As frequently happens with rising stars in the Church, McQuaid journeyed to Rome for further studies in theology. Rome made an immense impression on the young priest. He was fascinated by all of the great churches in the eternal city. His attachment to the papacy deepened, and he formed a special respect and love for St. Pius X. His theological training took place in the intellectual atmosphere that followed the repression of Modernism in the Catholic Church. He mistrusted the secularism ushered in by the French Revolution. He wanted no part of the "new" theology that developed in France and Germany following World War II.

While undergoing his religious training in Rome, McQuaid's great ambition was to become a missionary in Africa. He applied four times, but was turned down by his superiors. His talents were instead unleashed on Dublin and then later on all the Catholics of Ireland when he was appointed Archbishop of Dublin. On returning from Rome in 1925, John Charles was appointed to the staff of Blackrock College in Dublin. He was quickly promoted to dean of studies and became president of the college in 1931, serving in that capacity until the Vatican's *Congregation for Bishops* selected him as archbishop in 1940. As president at Blackrock, McQuaid was known as a strict taskmaster who reached out to help the less talented students. He made a name for himself as an administrator, serving as the elected chairman of the Catholic Headmasters Association from 1931 until 1940.

McQuaid's influence on the people of Ireland was not restricted to the Catholic population. While president of Blackrock College, he became good friends with one of the college's distinguished graduates, the popular Irish politician Eamon De Valera, known as Dev. Dev's wife, Sinead, was very active at the college where their two sons followed in their father's footsteps. McQuaid was a regular visitor at the De Valera home, which is very close to the college. He took advantage of Dev's attachment to the college to forge a personal relationship that survived many ups and downs over the next thirty or forty years.

According to John Cooney, author of *John Charles McQuaid: Ruler of Catholic Ireland*, "From 1937 Eamon De Valera was bombarded with letters, sometimes twice a day, from Father John McQuaid. They were crammed with suggestions, viewpoints, documents and learned references on what was to become the Constitution of Ireland."[4]

McQuaid's goal, to confirm the Catholic Church's absolute claim as the Church of Christ, was frustrated by then-*Taoiseach* De Valera. While some authors list John Charles as the co-author of the Irish Constitution, others strongly disagree. The fact remains that his influence was strong enough that the first words of the 1937 Constitution read: "In the Name of the Most Holy Trinity, from Whom all authority and to Whom, as our final end, all actions both of men and States must be referred"[5]

John Charles was the only Catholic bishop in Ireland to have a good relationship with Dev. The other bishops were distinctly cool to him. There is evidence in the Irish Government's archives, made public in 1990, that De Valera pressed the Vatican to make McQuaid the archbishop of Dublin. If De Valera later pushed the Vatican to elevate

John Charles to cardinal, it didn't happen, as the Vatican chose instead to elevate the archbishop of Armagh.

McQuaid was not only an influential politician, but was also a distinguished church leader who oversaw a phenomenal expansion of the church in the Archdiocese of Dublin. During his term as archbishop, forty-seven new parishes were established, with accompanying primary and secondary educational facilities. He created the Catholic Social Conference to regulate the several charitable organizations existing in the city.

From this point on in his career, John Charles received very different marks from his several biographers. In his 1974 book *John Charles McQuaid: the Man and the Mask*, John Feeney presents him as living outside his time and calls him a "first-class bishop of the old school," who, had he lived fifty years earlier, "would have no critics worth speaking about and would hardly be remembered except by those who benefited from his quiet personal charity."[6]

According to biographer John Cooney, McQuaid was a "power-hungry Renaissance style prelate."[7] Cooney does not include examples of McQuaid's quiet personal charity and "visiting hospitals after supper six nights a week," as described by Father Chris Mangan, McQuaid's secretary.[8]

To those whose primary interest is in seeing how McQuaid handled the Second Vatican Council, we are surprised to learn that, behind the formidable exterior, John Charles was an extremely shy person, ill at ease in social situations. When he traveled to Rome to participate in the first session of Vatican Council II in 1963, he was accompanied by several Irish bishops. I personally remember hearing a rumor that the archbishop's return to Dublin after the fourth session was met by a dozen or so reporters at Dublin International Airport. Their leader asked, "Your Excellency, what happened at the Council?" He replied abruptly, "NOTHING!" and proceeded with his chauffer to his limo.

To his credit, he set up an all-priest committee to examine what is now called the public image of the Church in the Dublin archdiocese. John Charles insisted that the committee members should not restrain their criticism, and they obliged. The committee reported that his public image was "entirely negative: a man who forbids, a man who doesn't want to meet people [as they want him to] at church functions, and public gatherings, or television or on the streets, who writes deep pastoral letters in theological and canonical language that is remote from the lives of the people."

He was obviously disappointed and hurt by the feedback. According to one of the committee members, he felt that the discussion focused too much on him personally. Most obviously, the priests on the committee and the laity they interviewed were more affected by the reported openness of the Vatican Council II discussion than their spiritual leader Archbishop McQuaid, even though he participated in the Council. Biographer Cooney notes that the archbishop will be remembered for his attempt at the end of the Council in 1965 to reassure his flock that "no change will worry the tranquility of your Christian lives."[9]

How wrong he was! There was no more tranquility in the Dublin archdiocese as priests and laity struggled to implement the liturgical changes unloosed by Pope John XXIII, reached out ecumenically to non-Catholic Christian churches, and then endured the storm raised by Pope Paul VI when he condemned artificial birth control.

It is clear from a study of the archbishop's papers that his attendance at the Council sessions in Rome was dutiful but without enthusiasm. He and his fellow Irish bishops were not prepared for the excitement generated by the first session of the Council. Upset about how the Irish religious correspondents reported the Council in the Irish newspapers, he told a priest friend that he was "dismayed by the facile ignorance of the journalists . . . writing about the documents that have cost us years of work . . . in regard to what we bishops must do."[10]

McQuaid actually implemented the decrees of Vatican II, including the ecumenical decrees. As a loyal churchman he was conflicted between loyalty to the Holy Father and the pain, for McQuaid, of Vatican II's requested transparency in the exercise of authority. Like many of his fellow bishops in Ireland and the world, he made the mistake of protecting the good name of the Church and the priests in his own archdiocese when he refused to allow one of his auxiliary bishops to report an archdiocesan pedophile priest to the police.[11]

The question remains: Did McQuaid's patrician background in County Cavan prevent his being more open to sharing his authority as a true servant-bishop like Angelo Roncalli? Or did his theological training in the repressive intellectual atmosphere of Rome reinforce an early tendency to be authoritarian? Or, in spite of his extraordinary intellectual prowess, did his shyness inhibit his style? Perhaps, if he had gone to the missions for ten or twenty years or experienced the challenges of being a pastor, he could have been the archbishop that Vatican II called for and the Irish Church needed.

CHAPTER X

Pope Benedict Offers Help to Ireland

Two issues regarding the life and ministry of Catholic priests have been headlines in secular papers in Ireland over the past ten years: the relevance of mandatory celibacy for priests in today's Church, and the healing needed to alleviate the hurt and anger caused by the pedophile crisis.

In an editorial in the *Irish Voice* on April 10, 2002, Niall Dowd wrote, "Here in Ireland the drip feed of allegations and lawsuits has become an emblem of how totally the Catholic Church has lost its bearings in a society the bishops once dominated with an iron fist." The previous Sunday headline in the popular *Irish Independent* read "Resign call to Cardinal after Euro400K Payout," a reference to the revelation that the Archdiocese of Dublin had paid compensation to victims of sexual abuse by one of Cardinal Desmond Connell's priests.[1]

Today the issue of mandatory celibacy is simple and relatively straightforward for many observers. Father Brian Darcy, a popular priest-author and radio broadcaster from the Passionist Order in Enniskillen, County Fermanagh, Northern Ireland, has commented, "We are losing good men."[2] When asked whether it was common for priests to fall in love, he said, "I would think that every priest worth his salt had to face it at least once in his life. Of course not all priests will break their vows. They have to make a difficult choice. How can any normal person go through forty or fifty years of their life and not fall in love? It is something

I had to face up to myself." Later he added, "It is a significant time to think (now) about the value of mandatory celibacy. This may have been suitable for a particular time but that time has now gone. Remember that the first pope, St. Peter, was married."

Richard Sipe, a psychiatrist at Johns Hopkins University in Baltimore, Maryland, has estimated that just 10 percent of priests are successfully celibate.[3] He contends that 50 percent have at some stage in their ministry been sexually active. Father Darcy believes celibacy can be a good thing, but it should be voluntary. Revelations from Dr. Sipe and Father Darcy do not cause the shock and handwringing that occurred in 1992 when it was revealed that Bishop Eamonn Casey from Galway fathered a son and then abandoned both mother and child for years. It was later revealed that Casey used Church funds to buy their silence.[4]

In 1993 the news also broke that the well-known Dublin priest Father Michael Cleary had fathered two children with his longtime housekeeper. Cleary had lived with his common-law wife and son while pretending that he was merely giving her employment and assistance. The secret emerged only when the housekeeper's gynecologist encouraged her to reveal the truth after Father Cleary's death.[5]

From the year 2000 forward, a few of the priests who were violating their vows of celibacy but still feeling the call to ministry have chosen to leave the Catholic Church and become clergymen in either the Church of Ireland, Anglican/Episcopal or one of the other Christian churches. In the same issue of the *Irish Independent* newspaper cited earlier in this chapter, a photo shows former Father Dermot Dunne, a Catholic priest who became a Church of Ireland clergyman, kissing his wife. Another picture shows Sean McKenna, a Catholic priest who left the Catholic Church to pursue a love affair. The faithful in Ireland have come to accept that priests might have consensual relationships with women. However, the growing fury of lay Catholics towards the hierarchy's handling of pedophile priests threatens to push Irish Catholicism over the brink. Niall Dowd concludes his *Irish Voice* editorial with, "It is not an exaggeration to conclude that the very survival of the Church as a meaningful institution is on the line."

The relatively new Archbishop of Dublin Diarmuid Martin is a fresh voice for the hierarchy in Ireland. In contrast to his predecessors

McQuaid and Connell, Martin is forthright in condemning the Irish Catholic congregations for concealing decades of child abuse.

Cardinal Sean Brady, the primate of the Irish Catholic Church, is remorseful on behalf of the total Catholic Church. He said, "We are ashamed, humbled and repentant that our people strayed away from their Christian ideals, for this we ask forgiveness. The abuses were the result of a culture that was prevalent in the Catholic Church in Ireland for far too long."[6] I interpret that latter statement to include a condemnation of the authoritarian, secretive and "defend the Church's good name at all costs" culture.

On March 20, 2010, Pope Benedict XVI issued a formal apology to the Irish sexual abuse victims and their families. He said, "I have been deeply disturbed by information which has come to light regarding the abuse of children and vulnerable young people by members of the Church in Ireland, particularly by priests and religious. I can only share in the dismay and the sense of betrayal that many of you have experienced on learning of these sinful criminal acts and the way the Church authorities in Ireland dealt with them."

Pope Benedict admitted that the decades of cover-up by the Church evidenced "a misplaced concern for the reputation of the Church and avoidance of scandal." He condemned bishops who colluded in the concealment of sex abuse cases, but, in the judgment of many listeners, his words were only in the vaguest of terms. He said that "Grave errors of judgment were made and failures of leadership occurred."[7]

The pope's letter to the Catholics of Ireland was published on the feast of St. Joseph, March 19, 2010. The Irish bishops used the letter at their annual meeting in October as the core of their initiative for healing and reconciliation. They scheduled a year of prayer, penance and spiritual renewal starting on the First Sunday of Advent, November 28, 2010. The laity was expected to pray, read the Scriptures and perform works of mercy as a means of healing and renewal for the Church of Ireland. The response from the Catholic laity was lukewarm at best.

Father Thomas Doyle, a Canon lawyer and advocate for those abused by priests, disagreed with the Irish bishops' solution, saying, "The Church cannot and will not fix itself. The very reality of the systemic abuse in the Irish institutions reveals a deep disdain for people by those charged with leading the Church. . . . There is something radically wrong with the institutional Catholic Church. This is painfully obvious because it allows systemic abuse and radical dishonesty to co-exist with its self-proclaimed identity as the Kingdom of God on earth. . . . [Believers] must ceaselessly do all that can be done to free the Christian/Catholic Church from the toxic control of the clericalized institutional structure so that once more the Church will be identified not with an anachronistic and self-serving monarchy but with the Body of Christ."[8]

In the same year, Liam McDaid, the newly appointed bishop of Clogher in County Monaghan, addressed the congregation present at his installation at St. McCartan's Cathedral on July 25, 2010. He said, "The surgeon's knife has been painful and necessary to rid the Catholic Church of the evil of clerical child abuse."[9]

Pope Benedict recognized that a pastoral letter to the Irish Catholic faithful was not enough to dispel the anger of sexual abuse victims and their families or the frustration of the average adult Catholic craving radical changes in the Church hierarchy. The pope appointed nine prelates, including the archbishops from Boston and New York, to investigate firsthand the child abuse crisis in Ireland. Cardinal Sean O'Malley of Boston was assigned to the Dublin archdiocese headed by Archbishop Diarmuid Martin.

Some Catholics in the United States would describe the O'Malley appointment as sending the fox to protect the hen house. Others felt the cardinal had done a good job since he took the place of Cardinal Law, who was forced out of Boston after he had merely moved pedophile priests to different places rather than reporting them as criminals to civil authorities. O'Malley, on the other hand, gained a positive reputation by apologizing to the sexual abuse victims, inviting them to healing liturgical rituals, settling their lawsuits and changing policies in the three scandal-racked dioceses he led. He actually arranged a meeting between the survivors and Pope Benedict XVI. At that meeting he presented the pope with a hand-lettered book containing the first names of 1,476 abuse victims.[10]

Archbishop Timothy M. Dolan of New York was assigned to investigate the training of future priests in the seminaries of Ireland. A report published in the *Irish Voice* on March 24, 2011, claimed that

Dolan was "appalled" at the standards at Maynooth College, Kildare, where students for the Irish dioceses had been prepared for centuries. Reportedly, Dolan recommended that the seminary be closed because of its lack of orthodoxy, and that all seventy-two seminarians be transferred to the Irish seminary in Rome. Shortly after the release of this devastating proposal, Monsignor Hugh Connolly, president of Maynooth College, announced that the "media reports of the closure of the seminary are without foundation." He added, "[Maynooth is] the largest seminary on these islands and one of the largest in Europe."[11]

David Clohessy, the executive director of the American group SNAP (Survivors Network of those Abused by Priests), is troubled that the hierarchy wants to expand its mission to evangelize Ireland. His view is that the Vatican should be addressing the issue of sexual abuse and the cover-up rather than worrying now about more people going to confession. Clohessy states, "Our goal and those of the laity and priests in the Church are the same, but the goals of the Church hierarchy are different."[12]

Of all the pope's emissaries to Ireland, Cardinal O'Malley gets the highest marks. Repeating what he initiated in his home Diocese of Boston, he and Archbishop Martin invited several victims of clergy sex abuse to a ritual healing in Dublin. O'Malley got down on his knees and washed the feet of the victims as a sign of the Church seeking forgiveness. Before he returned to Boston, he addressed the lay reform group People of God and said, "If the Church in Ireland does not give laymen and women a greater say in decision making, it is possible that in five or ten years it will lose its relevancy in Irish life." He estimated that, at most, the Irish Church had a decade to avoid falling over the edge and "becoming like other European countries where religion is marginal in society."[13]

Where is the hope for the Church of my fatherland? Just two years ago in Ireland, a new group was formed. The overall goal of this group, the Association of Catholic Priests, is to restore the Catholic Church to its post-Vatican II mindset of transparency in governing, sharing of decisions with lay members, both male and female, and restructuring the governing systems of the Church.

In particular, the Association's objectives include: the primacy of the individual conscience, the status and active participation of all the baptized, and the task of establishing a Church where all believers will be treated as equals. Father Hoban, one of the founding priests of the association, stated, "This was the reform policy that was called for by the Second Vatican Council when the world's bishops met in Rome from 1962 to 1965, but it has not been put into practice in Ireland."[14]

While pessimists view the present state of the Irish Church as catastrophic, positive progressive thinkers see great hope. Seeds of change are being sown at the bottom rung of the Church by lay groups like the People of God. Meanwhile, the newly formed Association of Catholic Priests may persuade sixty-five hundred of their fellow priests to join them in restoring the Irish Church to its traditional position of prominence in Irish society. Change, if and when it happens, will come from the bottom up.

Cardinal O'Malley Washes the Feet of a Victim in Dublin

CHAPTER XI

Archbishop Martin: A Breath of Fresh Air

For many years I have struggled with some basic questions about the Catholic Church and its administrative practices:

- *Why does the Congregation for Bishops, which oversees the selection of some new bishops, recommend candidates with little or no pastoral experience?*
- *Doesn't the Congregation know that the primary function of a bishop is to be a pastor to his flock?*
- *Why does the same Congregation exercise complete secrecy and total control when interviewing priests regarding a particular candidate?*
- *Why doesn't the laity have a say in selecting the new bishops who will serve them?*
- *Why are candidates for bishop required to take an oath that they will never support the ordination of women?*
- *Why is a similar negative oath required of all candidates for bishop, even though some of them believe that couples should follow their own conscience in selecting their family planning methods?*
- *Are the members of the Congregation for Bishops instructed to select safe, orthodox candidates versus candidates who are truly pastoral?*

- *Did Jesus intend to create a monarchical, hierarchical society whose power was primarily based in the pope and bishops?*
- *If that was His intention, why is it that today's non-Catholic Christian churches do not have a similar structure?*

Today's laity is much better educated and more sophisticated than it was two centuries ago when the rules and customs that govern celebration of the liturgy and appointment of bishops were established. It seems time for the laity to participate in the decisions that affect their parish life. If the hierarchy continues to shut out today's sophisticated laity, the consequences will be dire, and will shock positive thinkers who love the Church.

During the next twenty to twenty-five years, the present structures and disciplines of the Church must be reformed. Without substantial changes, many of the young, educated Catholics will abandon their Church. Some have already chosen other Christian denominations free from outdated hierarchical structures.

Despite this desertion, I feel hopeful for the Catholic Church of Ireland. The 2009 publications of the Ryan Report and the Murphy Report provoked a sudden change of attitude among the Irish laity and some priests. Archbishop of Dublin Diarmuid Martin exemplifies a new openness that can revitalize the Church. As reported in Chapter VII, the Murphy Report criticized the Archdiocese of Dublin for its "obsessive concern" with secrecy and avoidance of "scandal at all costs," with "little or no concern for the welfare of the abused child."

Although terribly upset by its conclusions, the recently appointed Archbishop Martin did not hide behind the religious doctrine of "mental reservation" to conceal the full truth and thus protect offending priests, even though his predecessors in the pre-Vatican II Church had done so. Martin provided seven hundred thousand pages of documents from the archdiocesan office to the Murphy committee in Dublin. He took responsibility for the harm it caused, changed the clerical culture that gave rise to the cover-up, and welcomed victims into the Church community.

On the day the Murphy Report was published, Martin held a press conference that can easily be labeled a confession: *"As Archbishop of a Diocese for which I have pastoral responsibility, of my own native diocese, of the diocese for which I was ordained a priest, of a Diocese which I love and hope to serve to the best of my ability, what can I say when I have to share with you the revolting story of sexual abuse and rape of so many young children and teenagers by priests of the Archdiocese or who ministered in the diocese? No words of apology will be sufficient.*"[1]

He followed up with a letter to the priests and laity of the Archdiocese that continued the apology: "*The damage done to children abused by priests can never be undone. As Archbishop of Dublin and as Diarmuid Martin I offer to each and every survivor my apologies, my sorrow and my shame for what happened to them. I am aware however that no words of apology will be sufficient.*"[2]

This open and contrite approach was in direct contrast to what he and Cardinal Sean Brady experienced when they met to discuss the Murphy Report with Pope Benedict XVI and a host of Curial officials, including, among others, the cardinal secretary of state, the apostolic nuncio to Ireland, and cardinal prefects of the Congregations of the Clergy, Bishops, Doctrine of the Faith and Institutes of Consecrated Life.

That meeting was both a communication and problem-solving disaster. The discussion, or debate, or whatever you wish to label it, missed the focus highlighted by Martin's expression of shame, sorrow and apology to the victims. Instead it focused on the negativity of the Irish media toward the Murphy Report. One commentator summarized the two-day meeting as a "dialogue between deaf parties."[3] The inability of the Curial officials to deal with the truth of the child abuse tragedy reminded me of a scene in one of my favorite movies, *A Few Good Men*, when Jack Nicholson screamed at Tom Cruise, "You cannot handle the truth." Apparently, the Vatican has a similar problem with the truth.

The Vatican meeting would have dulled anyone's hopes, especially if they were expecting the pope and the *Curia* to initiate reform. As already noted in Chapter I, the Vatican *Curia* members were threatened by any move toward reform because they saw it as a threat to their authority. It seems quite clear that change and renewal in the Church would have to come from the bottom up.

There is, however, reason for hope manifested by the manner in which the Vatican investigations took place in Ireland. Although it was customary for the Vatican to carry out its investigations in secret, Boston's Cardinal O'Malley, the prelate assigned to investigate sexual abuse in the Archdiocese of Dublin, chose a completely different approach. He openly invited abuse survivors and their families to join him and Archbishop Martin in a Liturgy of Lament and Repentance.[4]

Like Martin, O'Malley didn't cite "mental reservation" or blame the Irish media for negative reporting. Instead, he knelt down with Archbishop Martin and washed the feet of several sexual abuse survivors, one victim's mother, and another victim's spouse. Addressing the victims, their families and local clergy, O'Malley called on senior Irish church officials to turn a new page and, speaking directly to them, said, "We want to be part of the Church that puts survivors, the victims of abuse first, ahead of self-interest, reputation and institutional needs." Victim Darren McGavin was very moved by the two bishops' actions and said, "I found it hard to forgive, but today I found a small bit of closure."[5]

Father Tony Flannery, one of the three priest-founders of the Association of Catholic Priests, highly praised Cardinal O'Malley for "really listening." He added that Martin and O'Malley grasp "the depth and urgency of the crisis in Ireland generated by revelations of decades of sexual abuse and cover up," and they have placed "no restrictions on the conversation about reform."[6]

The only significant negative report on any of the visitors stemmed from Archbishop Timothy Dolan's mishandling of his role as a visitor to the seminaries in Ireland. Allow me to be kind to a fellow priest, even though Dolan would not have been my choice for such a sensitive assignment. In a 2011 interview on *60 Minutes*, a national television program, Dolan first admitted that the sexual abuse scandal by Catholic priests was a cancer in the Church. He then demonstrated that he was incapable of getting away from the Vatican party line. When the interviewer asked him about possible reforms in Church discipline, like optional celibacy or ordination of women, Dolan laughed.

The archbishop was also asked what changes were necessary to meet the demands from Catholics alarmed by the pedophilia disaster and convinced of the need for radical change. Dolan admitted that the argument for married priests was popular, but that it would not change the longstanding decision of the Church. He finally admitted that his goal was to persuade all the faithful Catholics to embrace the permanence and stability of the Catholic Church's teaching.

When Archbishop Dolan visited the centuries-old seminary of Maynooth, County Kildare, he reviewed some notes the seminarians provided and came to the conclusion that the students were not getting adequate training. He then quickly leaped to the judgment that the seminary should be closed and that all the Irish seminarians should be transferred to the Irish Seminary in Rome.[7]

Why did the archbishops in both Ireland and the United States handle the crisis so differently? Why can't the hierarchy in both countries see that clericalism, secrecy and authoritarianism are the cancer in the Church that has created an opportunity for cover-ups of the pedophile priests?

As an Irish-born priest, I am very proud of Archbishop Diarmuid Martin's strong leadership. Speaking at a sexual abuse conference at Marquette University in April 2011, Martin told the participants that the only way for the Catholic Church to truly emerge from the abuse crisis is to divulge all of its secrets. I like the Martin mantra "The truth will set us free." He is not waiting for the Vatican to issue renewal directives. He has already instituted changes in the seminary to develop more priests who see themselves as equal to rather than above the laity.[8] It is my hope that the Marquette conference attendees and Martin's colleague bishops back home in Ireland will listen to Martin's sage advice.

Ian Elliott, chief executive officer of Ireland's National Board for Safeguarding Children in the Catholic Church, complained that Church officials have resisted requests to open their files to outside scrutiny. Quoting Archbishop Martin, Elliott repeated, "*The truth will set us free,*" and then added, "*but I also believe that continued secrecy will enslave us forever.*"[9]

CHAPTER XII

The Netherlands Embraces Vatican Council II

Leaving the Church of Ireland and moving to Holland, we discover a very different Church, thanks to a renowned Dominican scholar named Edward Schillebeeckx who taught theology in Holland for more than five decades. His teachings and many writings prepared the Catholic population of the Netherlands for the openness and dialogue with other faiths initiated by Pope John XXIII at Vatican Council II.

His first book, *Christ the Sacrament of the Encounter with God*, challenged the theology I was raised with in Ireland, where I was taught that the sacraments, in an almost mechanical way, dispensed grace to the recipients. Schillebeeckx stressed that the sacraments were, in fact, interactive meetings with Jesus. Father Robert Schreiter, the leading expert on Schillebeeckx, teaches theology at Catholic Theological Union in Chicago. He wrote that Schillebeeckx believed that normal Catholic people should be able to see a measure of reasonableness in Catholic teaching and be able to link their experiences with the revealed traditions of the Christian faith.[1]

Schillebeeckx was a different kind of theologian in many ways. He didn't merely follow the words in Scripture and the dictates of the Vatican; he was interested in seeing how people experienced Jesus. Above all else, Schillebeeckx was an advocate of personal theology and its pastoral implications for individuals and the faith community.

When plans for Vatican Council II were announced, Schillebeeckx was ready and coauthored a statement, signed by seven Dutch bishops. He actually forecast all of the progressive changes that came out of the Council, like Liturgy, Ecumenism, Dialogue with other Faiths, and encouragement of the hierarchy to share authority and discussions on church discipline with lay Catholics. Many progressive theologians were surprised that Schillebeeckx was not invited as a *peritus*. He did, however, work closely with his country's spiritual leader, Cardinal Bernard Alfrink of Utrecht, and other participants at the Council. Schillebeeckx placed emphasis on the collegial nature of the episcopacy as a balance to papal infallibility, pronounced at Vatican Council I in 1869-70. While attendees at the Vatican Council debated and made decisions that would eventually affect all Catholics, Schillebeeckx joined fellow theologians Hans Kung, Karl Rahner and Yves Congar in launching a new theological journal called *The Concilium.*

As reported in Chapter III, the enthusiasm for Vatican II changes effected by Vatican Council II cooled among the Vatican staff after the death of Pope John XXIII. The Vatican *Curia* saw all this sharing of authority with bishops and laity as a threat to their authority. They were not emotionally prepared to lose or share the authority they had accumulated in the ninety years since Vatican Council I.

The Catholic Church of the Netherlands was not dissuaded from its movement. In 1966 they formed the Dutch Pastoral Council, a group of fifty-six clergy and laity elected by the diocesan parish councils. Another twenty-eight members were chosen by the Pastoral Council itself. The Pastoral Council raised issues and held discussions on homosexuality, contraception, married priests, and more democracy in the church hierarchy.

Even though the leadership made lengthy and elaborate preparations, it never really got off the ground. The *Congregation for the Clergy*, obviously threatened by the independence and possible threat to Vatican authority, declared that members of the Pastoral Council should be appointed by the bishop and not elected, should not have a permanent character, and should not present itself as representing the body of the faithful. The Congregation asserted, "All believers have a right and a duty to take an active part in the mission given to the

Church . . . but they have neither a right nor a duty to give advice to the hierarchy in the exercise of their pastoral task."[2]

That last paragraph put the final nail in the coffin of the best possible movement to bring the Church up to date with modern society. The response from the laity was divided. Progressives, who regarded Vatican II as a launching pad for a brave new Church, looked upon the activities of the Pastoral Council as the wave of the future. Conservatives saw what was happening in the Netherlands as nothing less than a Second Reformation.

What effect did Vatican Council II have on the religious practices of clergy and laity in the Netherlands? Michael Gilchrist, author of "Growth of a 'new church': a Dutch experiment," writes: "During the 1950s the Netherlands possessed a higher ratio of priests and religious to Catholic populations than any other European country. Its Sunday Mass attendance rate was among the highest in the world at the time of the Council; as late as 1967 the figure was still 63 per cent, including 84 per cent in rural areas. The Dutch's church missionary activity before Vatican II was unequalled in the world: with 2 per cent of the world's Catholics, it provided 11 per cent of the world's missionary priests."[3]

What happened as a result of the condemnation of the Dutch Pastoral Council of the Netherlands by the *Congregation for the Clergy*? Post-Vatican II conservatives like Ralph M. McInerny, author of *What Went Wrong with Vatican II: The Catholic Crisis Explained*, blame Vatican II for the drop in church attendance and the dramatic decrease in religious vocations to the priesthood and convents.[4] Progressives like Michael Gilchrist give a different analysis, blaming the *Congregation for the Clergy's* condemnation of the pastoral council in the Netherlands. He states: "Yet within scarcely ten to fifteen years there was almost a complete collapse. For example, between 1960 and 1970 ordinations to the priesthood fell from 318 to 16, a far worse drop than in the neighboring Belgium or West Germany. Mass attendance fell to less than 20 per cent of the pre-Vatican II high of 70-75 per cent; again, a much worse decline than elsewhere. During the same period 4,300 nuns and brothers left religious life and over 2,000 secular priests defected or were laicized; this was three times the world average."[5]

Meanwhile the Vatican grew more hostile toward Schillebeeckx, criticizing his most influential work, *Jesus: An Experiment in Christology*, and stating that its orthodoxy was questionable. He was summoned to Rome by the *Congregation for the Doctrine of the Faith* in 1984 and again in 1985. During the second visit, the Congregation questioned Schillebeeckx regarding his views on the resurrection of Jesus Christ and his understanding of ministry in the Church. Yet they never charged him or found him guilty of heresy.

During the same period, an anonymous progressive group in the Netherlands sent a booklet to all the parishes in Holland. Although not directly linked to Schillebeeckx, the booklet clearly reflected his theological reasoning and was approved by the Dominican Province. The booklet's author reasoned that, because of the scarcity of priests today, Catholic parishes should begin selecting members who would preside over the Eucharist, as was the custom in the early Church. The Dominicans knew this practice was illegal, but they based their endorsement of the booklet on something Schillebeeckx had written in his book *The Church with a Human Face: A new and expanded Theology of Ministry.*

The Vatican was anxious for good reason. The Catholic Church in Holland was ready for a schism. The papacy and the Vatican were viewed with hostility or disdain. In turning against the Vatican, the Dutch Catholics further increased their involvement with other non-Catholic groups.

Meanwhile the Netherlands' hierarchy acted in similar fashion to the bishops in Ireland and the U.S. who were shielding pedophile priests. Cardinal Adrianus Simonis got into trouble with the State when he failed to report a priest who had molested a boy, as reported to him by his auxiliary bishop. Incidentally, this cardinal was the same orthodox bishop appointed by Pope Paul VI in 1970 to the Rotterdam diocese to counteract the liberal Catholic elite in the Netherlands.

It is a coincidence that Simonis followed the same practice of shielding pedophile priests as Cardinal Bernard Law did in the Archdiocese of Boston. Simonis sent the pedophile priest to receive psychological counseling and later transferred him to another parish based on the psychological report he received. Both cardinals were following the then-current instructions from the Vatican on dealing with pedophile priests, which included ignoring the criminality of the offense. Almost two thousand people have made complaints of sexual abuse against the Church in the Netherlands, a country of only four million Catholics.

In 1983 Pope John Paul II radically tilted the balance toward orthodoxy and loyalty to Rome by appointing three conservative bishops to the three largest Dutch dioceses. These appointments had little effect in blocking the growth of the "New Church" made up of professionals and bureaucrats.

The drama between the Vatican and the New Church in the Netherlands continued during the reign of John Paul II, who was known as the travelling pope because of his more than one hundred visits to foreign countries. His advisors encouraged him to visit the Netherlands in 1985 to support the conservative bishops he had appointed. Some journalists called his trip "John Paul's Dutch misadventure."

The organizers, led by Cardinal Simonis, were disappointed from the beginning of his four-day visit. Several thousand people were expected to greet him as he walked down the gangway of the papal plane to kiss the ground at Utrecht Airport. Instead there were only a few hundred. Several protesters manned the city streets and yelled anti-Vatican statements. Once the pope and his entourage were escorted inside the Cathedral, calmness and then loud applause greeted him.

Another surprise awaited His Holiness and Cardinal Simonis. While all of the greeters read their approved texts to the pope, one reader, Ms. Hedwig Wasser, read part of her approved text but then suddenly stopped and stared towards the pope as she asked, "Do we present a credible version of the Gospel message if we preach with raised finger in place of an outstretched hand? If there is no room for . . . but in fact an exclusion of . . . discussion on married partners, divorce, marriage in the priesthood, and homosexuals?" At the conclusion of John Paul's four-day visit, Cardinal Simonis reportedly said, "There has never been a day that I breathed such a wonderful sigh of relief than when he boarded the plane and took off for Luxemburg."[6]

In 1988 Father Bots, the Jesuit theologian and sociologist, described the unraveling of the Dutch Church: "If Catholicism has not been totally extinguished, it is because the Church in Holland had considerable spiritual reserves. But nowhere in the world has a branch of the Church so squandered and corrupted its Catholic heritage in the name of post-conciliar renewal," with the minority Orthodox Catholics exiled to a kind of "spiritual Diaspora existence" within their own Church. He continued, "Disparaged as conservative, rigid, intolerant, extreme or dogmatic, their [the Dutch hierarchy's] influence on the day-to-day running of the Church is effectively nil. Otherwise, there are but small oases of untainted Catholicism, notably some Benedictine communities." In recent decades the number of Catholics in the Netherlands has continued to decrease as a percentage of the population by approximately half a percent annually, from 40 percent in the 1970s to 26 percent in 2007. Even so, the Dutch Catholic Church still remains the largest religious group in the country.[7]

CHAPTER XIII

The Pope versus Belgium

Archbishop Andre-Joseph Leonard of Mechelin-Brussels, Belgium, shocked the Belgian Parliament's Commission on Child Sexual Abuse on December 22, 2010, when he proclaimed that "he saw no reason for the Church to compensate victims of sexual abuse" by clergy. He said "The civil court must determine the compensation and the offender must pay."[1]

This arrogant declaration was in direct contrast to the humble, contrite statement of his predecessor Cardinal Godfred Daneels. On the previous day, Daneels told the commission that the Church must react with humility and make some profound gestures, including compensation. He added, "For too long the Church thought only of itself and about its priests and now it is time to think about the victims of sexual abuse."[2]

To say that the commission was alarmed at Leonard's testimony is a gross understatement. Outraged, commission member Stefan Van Hecke said, "This is pure provocation and I am shocked." Leonard remained defiant and at times was sarcastic, replying to Van Hecke with "What, you think I have never been attacked?"[3] Leonard's former press officer Jürgen Mettepesnnmingen said of his old boss's testimony, "This is incomprehensible and very painful."[4] When he had resigned from his job with Leonard, Mettepesnnmingen compared Leonard's leadership to a reckless driver going in the wrong direction.[5]

Over the Christmas and New Year holidays, three of Leonard's fellow Belgian bishops (Bonny, De Kessel, and Hoogmartens) began speaking out in support of the victims of sexual abuse by priests. Their activity probably caused Leonard to change his defensive attitude. Bishop Johan Bonny, in words similar to those used by Archbishop Martin from Dublin, stated, "We want to and have to come clean with the past."[6] Meanwhile an independent commission appointed by the bishops of Belgium reported 475 cases of abuse of minors over the past several decades. Pope Benedict was obviously not aware of Leonard's arrogant testimony before the commission, or otherwise he would not have appointed Leonard to the newly established Pontifical Council for Promoting Evangelization.

Archbishop Andre-Joseph Leonard was not the only bishop to draw unfavorable attention with respect to how he mishandled the priest-pedophile disaster in Belgium. On Friday, April 23, the longest-serving bishop in Belgium, Bishop Roger Vangheluwe of Bruges, resigned after admitting to sexually abusing a boy he first described as "a boy in my close entourage." The Vatican issued a statement saying that Vangheluwe, who had been bishop of Bruges for twenty-five years, admitted that the abuse occurred when "I was still a simple priest and for awhile after I began as bishop." The bishop reportedly had asked the victim and his family several times for forgiveness, but added that the wound had not healed "neither in me or the victim." What the bishop didn't reveal until later was that the first victim was his own nephew, and that he had also sexually abused a second nephew for a brief period.[7]

The year 2010 was very painful for both the pope and the Vatican, painful enough that the Holy Father could use the memorable words of Queen Elizabeth II of the United Kingdom to describe the trauma created by the hierarchy in Europe . . . *Annus Horribilis.* Bishops all over the world were resigning, either because they were accused of covering up for pedophile priests, or because they themselves physically or sexually abused children. On the same day that the Vatican accepted the resignation of Bishop Vangheluwe, they also accepted the resignation of Bishop Moriarty of the Diocese of Kildare and Leighlin in Ireland. Moriarty had been cited in the Irish Government's report for mishandling and concealing sex abuse by priests while he served as auxiliary bishop in the Archdiocese of Dublin. Bishop Walter Mixa, one of the most conservative bishops in Germany, resigned because he was accused of physically abusing children decades earlier. In April Norwegian Bishop George Mueller, who had stepped down in May 2009, admitted that he had resigned because he had sexually abused a boy in the 1990s.

As reported earlier in this chapter, Bishop Roger Vangheluwe resigned in 2010. To the surprise of many, Archbishop Andre-Joseph Leonard took charge of the situation at a press conference in Brussels. First, he praised Bishop Vangheluwe as "a generous and dynamic bishop,"[8] but then he added, "We are aware of the crisis of confidence his resignation will set in motion." He admitted that the Church of Belgium needed to make a dramatic change to "turn over a new leaf from a not-so-distant past when such matters would pass in silence or be concealed." Archbishop Leonard made a total conversion from being defensive of the Church's good name and protective of its finances to following the example of Archbishop Martin of Dublin, who focused first on the victims of sexual abuse by clergy and then advocated telling the truth to initiate the process of healing in the Church of Belgium.

Catholic bishops and priests have always been known as good preachers, particularly after the reformation of the Liturgy following Vatican Council II. The same cannot be said about their ability to communicate effectively on sensitive issues that might damage the faith of lay people, who hold their bishops and priests in high regard. A subsequent interview involving Roger Vangheluwe demonstrates the potential of a mistimed and poorly executed interview that caused damage to the faithful Catholics of Belgium.

Following his resignation, Vangheluwe left Belgium for several months of spiritual and psychological counseling. Then suddenly he appeared at a television studio connected to the Flemish channel VT4, where, dressed in an open shirt, he insisted on being interviewed to be simulcast to the Belgium faithful. What happened during the disastrous interview prompted a storm of negative criticism from several public officials in Belgium.[9]

Vangheluwe began by expressing his guilt for sexually abusing his two nephews. What surprised his audience was that he failed to admit that his actions were crimes or sins. When asked about continuing in the priesthood, he adamantly stated his intent to stay in the priesthood unless the Vatican forced him to leave.

Continuing the interview, he said, "I have been involved with children [for most of my priesthood] and I never felt the slightest attraction. It was a certain intimacy that took place." Then he proceeded in a tone and manner typical of a Sunday homily. He asked, "How did it happen? "As with all families, when they came to visit, the nephews slept with me. It began as a game with the boys. It was never a question of rape, there was never physical violence used. He never saw me naked and there was no penetration."[10]

Seemingly, he had forgotten that he was on national television, and, even worse, he failed to demonstrate any concern about the faith of his Catholic audience and their vulnerability. To no one's surprise, the Vatican did not respond immediately.

Stefaan De Clerck, Belgium's justice minister, didn't wait for the Vatican to make the first move. Moved by the negative effect the former bishop's words had on the Catholic population in Belgium, De Clerck called on the Vatican to impose a tough punishment on Vangheluwe for his insensitive and inappropriate behavior. De Clerck announced on RTL radio, "It should be much more severe than what has been imposed until now."[11]

During the unauthorized interview, Vangheluwe argued that in his relationship with his two nephews he was not driven by sexual motives. Then he proceeded with a statement of denial that would make any listener question whether he was a rational person. He asserted, "I don't have the impression at all that I am a pedophile. It was really just a small relationship. I don't have the feeling that my nephew was against it . . . quite the contrary."[12]

What was he actually saying here—that his nephews were equal partners with him in the sexual crime? Politicians (including the Belgian prime minister), lawyers representing sexual abuse victims, and parliamentary officials serving on sexual abuse committees—all were outraged. Karine Lalieux, the Belgian deputy leading the sexual abuse committee, was most expressive. She stated, "I say it is disgusting. Mr. Vangheluwe neither has understood that he committed crimes nor that he has minimized and relativised these crimes. I think of the victims and their suffering." A lawyer for dozens of victims who claim they have been abused by clergy stated, "I think it is astonishing that this man does not feel any guilt. . . . He is saying the victims enjoyed this and there is no feeling of regret at all."[13]

Walter Van Steenbrugge, a lawyer representing the two abused nephews, said that neither nephew wanted to comment. The Bishops Conference in Belgium said they were "extremely shocked by the way Bishop Vangheluwe minimized and made excuses for his actions and the consequences for the victims, their families, church believers, and the entire society."[14] They added that the total tone of the interview completely contradicted the efforts in recent months to take the problem of sexual abuse seriously, to listen to the victims and take appropriate measures.

"If ever an occasion demanded immediate and severe response from the pope, Vangheluwe's interview last night is it," said BishopAccountability.org, an organization founded in 2003 that documents the abuse crisis in the Roman Catholic Church. The group said later that the pope's silence was baffling and inexcusable.[15] All of this turmoil created by Vangheluwe's interview added fuel to the on-going fiery conflict between the civil authorities in Belgium and the Vatican. If the Vatican officials were asked how this whole conflict started, they would quickly point a finger at the Belgian police for raiding the Catholic Church's offices in Brussels and holding several bishops hostage for nine hours. That raid on June 24, 2010, was an effort to find evidence of child abuse by priests. The Vatican's first response was "Shock," "a Violation," assumedly because priests were (and are) answerable only to a Higher Authority.

While the bishops were detained, the police drilled into the tombs of two deceased cardinals entombed in the Brussels Cathedral. Archbishop Leonard said the raid was worthy of a scene in the movie *The Da Vinci Code*. He added, "The justice system does its work and it has a right to carry out searches. Nevertheless I find it slightly surprising that it went so far as poking around in tombs."[16]

The Vatican complained formally to the Belgian ambassador to the Holy See. The response from the Belgium Bishop's Conference was not negative. They said there was a feeling of dialogue, not conflict, with the civil officials. The report said that "it was not a pleasant experience, but everything was handled very correctly."[17]

The police in Leuven, Belgium, went too far when they confiscated the files of child psychiatrist Peter Adriaenssens, who oversaw many of the victims of abuse. "This is most unusual," said Gerald Fogarty, professor of history and religious studies at Boston College. "Even with all the anger in Boston this did not happen."[18] The fact remains that investigative commission case files on about 475 victims of sexual abuse were confiscated from the child psychiatrist. When a similar confiscation of the records of the Interdiocesan Committee on Sexual Abuse in Belgium took place, the entire committee resigned in protest to the raid.

As a result of that trauma, what is happening to the Catholic Church in Belgium? According to Karel Ceule, a member of an alternative Catholic Christian Prayer community called *Ecclesia* (Greek: calling together), "Leonard is a symbol of an old conservative Church. . . . It doesn't work anymore. We have reached a stage where we don't accept that the priest has to be the go-between [for mankind and God]. We want to take charge of Baptisms and Communion."[19]

In Belgium "Don Bosco is one of about a dozen alternative Catholic Churches that have sprouted up and grown in the past two years," write religious reporter Doreen Cavajal of the *New York Times* and Rachel Donadio, contributing reporter from Rome. Why alternative churches? "They are an uneasy reaction to a combination of forces: a shortage of priests, closing of churches, dissatisfaction with the Vatican's appointments of conservative bishops and, more recently, dismay over the cover up of priestly sexual abuse."[20]

"'We are resisting a little like Gandhi,' says Johan Veys, a married former priest who performs baptisms and recruits newcomers for other tasks at Don Bosco." While recognizing that they are on a collision course with the Vatican and the hierarchy in Belgium, they say, "We press onward quietly without a lot of noise. It is important to have a community where people feel at home and can find peace and inspiration," says Veys.[21]

Reverend Federico Lombardi, director of the Vatican Press, reminds the Catholic Church of Belgium that only ordained priests can celebrate

Mass and preside over most sacraments (i.e., baptism and marriage). Addressing the Belgian bishops, he tells them that it is their responsibility to intervene and explain to the alternative parishes "what is in order and out of order if one belongs to the Catholic Church." The primate of Belgium, Archbishop Leonard, is gun-shy about joining Lombardi publicly in addressing the alternative parishes. He recently created a conflict with the State when he criticized Belgian officials for prosecuting elderly pedophile priests and called it "Vengeance."[22]

Speaking in general about the state of the Church in Belgium, Reverend Gabriel Ringlet, a priest and former rector of the Catholic University of Louvain, which today is considering dropping "Catholic" from its name, says, "I think the Belgian Catholic Church is starting to feel something exceptional for the first time in forty years. A lot of Catholics are waking up and speaking out."[23] Only time will tell if the alternative parishes, where lay people now lead the congregation in celebrating the Eucharist, will succeed. Is this the beginning of a structural renewal of Catholicism? Or is it merely a cultural revolution that will leave the Catholic Church of Belgium in schism?

CHAPTER XIV

Australian Catholicism before and after Vatican II

While preparing for the priesthood at St. Patrick's College, Carlow, from 1954 until 1960, I remember scanning all of the class pictures of priests ordained at the Cathedral of the Assumption, Carlow, over the previous forty or fifty years. The majority were destined for English-speaking dioceses outside Ireland. I recall pictures and names of men with determined faces going to dioceses I had never heard of, such as Perth and Adelaide in Australia. There were also names of dioceses and archdioceses that were more familiar to me like Melbourne and Sydney. I remember that two students in the class ahead of me, Barney Maxwell and Joe Brown, signed up to serve in the Archdiocese of Melbourne. Joe Hynan, a member of our class, signed up for Melbourne and has been serving there for fifty years.

According to the 2006 Australian National Census, there were 5,126,000 Catholics in Australia, representing 25.8 percent of the total population.[1] Many of them were descendants of the Irish who were forced to emigrate during the failure of the potato crop that led to the great Irish Famine from 1845 to 1852. The rest of the immigrant population came to Australia prior to 1986 from the United Kingdom, many of them members of the Anglican Church. I remember seeing some Australian bishops or their delegates coming to our seminary in search of additional priests to serve their ever-increasing Catholic population. After World War II, six and one-half million people immigrated to Australia, not from the United Kingdom or Ireland, but from Italy, Malta, Lebanon, the Netherlands, Germany, Croatia, and Hungary. Today's immigrants to Australia come primarily from Asia and the Middle East.[2]

The first priests who ministered to the Catholics of Australia were from Ireland. I hesitate to report that they came as convicts. One of these priests, James Dixon, arrived in 1803 and was granted conditional emancipation and permission to say Mass for the Catholics in Sydney, a practice that he continued for one year until Governor King withdrew his privileges, forcing him to return, against his will, to Ireland. Mass was not celebrated in Australia again until 1820 when two English-born priests, John Joseph Therry and Philip Connolly, were appointed chaplains by the governor of London. Their arrival marked the beginning of the formal establishment of the Catholic Church in Australia.[3]

Following the arrival of Therry and Connolly, a significant development took place. Catholic schools were established in Australia. By 1833 there were about ten schools, all of which received financial assistance from the government. Unfortunately, this benefit was discontinued in 1872 when every state in Australia passed a law removing state aid from Catholic schools, thus presenting the Catholic Church with its first real crisis. The bishops, priests and laity decided to preserve the mini-Catholic school system. With little money available to pay teachers or create textbooks, they had no other choice but to appeal to the religious orders in Ireland and other European countries for help. In a very short time, help arrived from religious orders like the Jesuits and the Sisters of Charity.[4] The religious sisters set up schools, not only in major cities but also throughout the countryside. They provided Catholic education to the children of the Australian bush as well.

Catholicism in Australia blossomed after World War II. The number of Catholics grew rapidly and attendance at Sunday masses "was admirable."[5] There was a striking resemblance between my upbringing as a young Catholic boy in Ireland and the lives of Catholic families in Australia during this period. At home we said the nightly Rosary and abstained from meat on Fridays, and many adult Catholics belonged to church organizations like the men's Holy Name Society or the women's Rosary Society.

The Catholic Church gained more influence in Australia, as "Catholic charitable organizations, hospitals, and schools played a prominent role in welfare and education in Australia ever since colonial times." Prime Minister Kevin Rudd said at Catholic World Day 2008 in Sydney, "It was the church that began first schools for the poor. It was the church that began first hospitals for the poor. It was the church that began first refuges for the poor and these great traditions continue for the future."[6]

It is unfortunate that the prime minister's "prophecy" didn't turn out exactly as he had forecast. As indicated in earlier chapters about Church tensions in other countries, there developed in the Australian Catholic Church a similar tension between the conservative Catholics (both clerical and lay) supported by the *Curia* at the Vatican and progressive Catholics, who felt that the Church should adapt to the needs of today's society.

"The energies of Catholic Australians in recent years have been absorbed by contradictory approaches to being faithful. The first is the Church's institutional integrity (requirements of obedience, orthodoxy and conformity), the second is moral integrity (what should it be doing, by whom and how?)."[7] Popes John Paul II and Benedict XVI have both attempted to strengthen the Church against the influences of secularism by insisting on stricter disciplines for the clergy and laity and on a greater acceptance of the official teachings of the *Magisterium* by the faithful.

The reality in Australia is different, as several bishops, priests and thousands of Australian laity regard the declining numbers at Sunday masses, the dramatic drop in vocations to the priesthood and religious life, and the scandal of sexual abuse by priests as compelling reasons to move away from the old ways of the pre-Vatican II Church and to demand fundamental reform. Unfortunately, the rift between progressives and conservatives has reached a crisis stage, sometimes with disastrous consequences. If a progressive bishop proposes reform, the conservative groups in his diocese, (nicknamed the "the temple police") report what they believe to be their erring bishop to the Vatican.[8]

The rural Diocese of Toowoomba, Queensland, covers three hundred thousand square miles and only has a relative handful of healthy priests to cover thirty-five parishes. William Morris, the popular sixty-seven-year-old bishop, was the most recent casualty in the conflict between progressive and conservative Catholics in his own diocese and at the Vatican. Morris' supporters describe him as, "a bishop who takes a highly consultative approach to leadership, occasionally surveying church members to learn their opinion on various issues and consulting with members of parishes before appointing a new pastor." In his 2006 pastoral letter he raised the issues of ordaining women to the priesthood, ordaining married men and recognizing other Christian denominations' ordinations as possible solutions to the priest shortage.

The temple police felt they had adequate reason to report him to the pope. His approach apparently annoyed both the temple police in his own diocese and the *Curia* and *Congregation for Bishops in Rome.*[9] The Vatican had no legitimate reason to punish Bishop Morris for any of his actions, as he was merely following the teaching of the Vatican II Documents.

Take notice, Morris was not advocating these changes. He was only listing them as topics for discussion. Several months later he received notice that the *Congregation for Bishops* was conducting an investigation. The conservative Archbishop of Philadelphia Charles Chaput was sent to the Diocese of Toowoomba to conduct a "visitation." He met with Morris, his Council of Priests, diocesan officials and lay Catholics. Chaput let Morris know by fax that he had sent his report to the *Congregation for Bishops.*

The report was not published, and Morris does not have access to it. In a letter that was read at all the masses in his diocese on May 1, 2011, Morris wrote: "I have never seen the report prepared by the Apostolic Visitor. Without due process it has been impossible to resolve these matters, denying me natural justice without the possibility of appropriate defense and advocacy on my behalf."[10]

When reporters posed a list of questions to Chaput by e-mail, he responded, "Any apostolic visitation is governed by strict confidentiality. This is for the benefit of both parties involved." Asked in a follow up e-mail if the report he submitted would be released should Morris wish to make it public, he repeated his response that apostolic visitations are confidential.[11]

The reaction by the faithful in the Diocese of Toowoomba was a "groundswell of support." The National Council of Priests in Australia released a statement on May 3, 2011, saying they were "appalled at the lack of transparency and due process" and were "embarrassed by the shabby treatment meted out to an outstanding pastor of this diocese."

The popular bishop, who loves his Church, was more sad than angry at his treatment. While being interviewed on a public radio station he said, "I believe the Church is at its best when it is most transparent, when the eyes of Justice and the eyes of the Gospel are so clear that all rights are respected for individuals, no matter who they are in the community." He added that "the Church is damaged when we are not so open, when we are not so clear, when we are not allowing the openness to be able to be seen in the way we deal with things . . . in the way we give justice to people."[12] After eighteen years as bishop, it all came to an abrupt end with one stroke of the papal pen. It is clear that in today's hierarchical structure any attempt to democratize the Church is met with absolute rejection.

The focus of the post-Vatican II Church in Australia is on evangelization and a dialogue with the modern world. Progressive Catholics like the new definition of the Church as "The People of God" enunciated in the Vatican II document *Lumen Gentium,* and not simply the hierarchical structure. As the priests and laity incorporated the new vernacular liturgy and shared authority together at the parish level, new styles of ministry were created in the Church. One group led by Father Ted reached out to a large aboriginal population. Father Frank Brennan, a Jesuit and a lawyer, founded UNIYA, a center for human rights research, advocacy, education and networking. The Prime Minister of Australia, Paul Keating, was not impressed. He called Brennan the "meddling priest." Father Chris Reilly formed Youth off the Streets, a community organization that caters to homeless youth, the drug dependent, and those recovering from substance abuse.

How has all this post-Vatican II enthusiasm affected the men and women in the congregation? Unfortunately, it has not stopped the "desertion of the pews" similar to the drop in attendance at Sunday masses in Ireland, Belgium, and the Netherlands. From 1976 to 2006 the attendance at Sunday masses in Australia dropped from 50 percent to lower than 14 percent. The laity doesn't feel as attached to their local church as they did back in the early 1900s. They don't contribute as generously to the collection plate. Many see a disconnect between their lives and the local church.[13]

Chris McGillion, a former religious affairs editor for the *Sydney Morning Herald*, wrote a very insightful article for the *National Catholic Reporter* entitled "Morale falters in the Australian Church." He claims that the behavior of the temple police, who attend church, has had a very negative effect on the perception of the Church because they "have taken it upon themselves to patrol the boundaries of orthodoxy by spying on priests and bishops and reporting what they consider to be questionable behavior to Rome. Such reports are believed to have played a major role in shaping perceptions about the Church in this country among senior Vatican officials, including the current pope."[14]

In 1998 many of the Australian bishops participated in the Synod for Oceania in Rome and spoke to Vatican officials, including Ratzinger, about the need for Church reform that responded to the signs of the times. Once again the failure to follow through on Vatican Council II Documents and to begin a mature dialogue with these bishops was a missed opportunity for the Vatican officials. What these bishops got instead was an order to sign a document entitled *Statement of Conclusions,* which stated that the crisis of faith that exists in Australia was caused by the tolerance of Australian society, which in turn "led to religious indifference, distorted understandings of the faith and a 'blurring of the lines' between the roles of clergy and laity."[15]

I fail to see the logic of these conclusions. Furthermore, none of these Vatican mandates, according to McGillion, "has reversed the dramatic decline in the ranks of the religious orders or diocesan priests." The morale among priests is low. One forty-seven-year-old priest told McGillion that the only thing he ever wanted to do was to become a priest but that "given the state of the church today I look forward to the night when I go to sleep and just don't wake up."[16]

The morale among bishops is not better: "Bishop Chris Toohey, a charismatic leader and environmental pioneer resigned as head of the vast rural Diocese of Wilcania-Forbes in July 2009 without explanation. . . . Bishop Michael John Malone, age 71, took early retirement because he said, 'I toss and turn at night over sex abuse committed by clergy and I experience a lot of anxiety.' Auxiliary bishop Pat Power of Canberra admitted publicly that he was thinking seriously of retiring at age 70. He said he wanted out of administration and into a pastoral appointment, but insiders say Power . . . generally regarded as mildly progressive . . . is frustrated in dealing with the deaf ears of Vatican officials."[17]

McGillion concludes, referring to the Church in Australia, that "we are not unique. We are also experiencing the failure of an old model of church and the stunting of the birth of the new."

On a positive note, the *Congregation for Bishops* recognized the changing face of the Australian Church when they selected a Vietnamese priest, Vincent Long Van Nguyen, as the first Asian-born priest and ordained him auxiliary bishop of Melbourne on June 23, 2011.[18] This action gives hope to the Australian Church and will assist Asian Catholics in significantly impacting the birth of a new Catholic Church in Australia. On the day of his ordination as bishop, Van Nguyen joyfully reflected on his journey from North Vietnam to Australia, saying, "It was a twist of fate that I followed the footsteps of my parents who themselves took to the sea to escape Communism in North Vietnam."[19]

CHAPTER XV

The Universal Church and Germany Lag Behind

In 1969, five years after Vatican Council II concluded, Missouri teenager David Clohessy came forward, a victim of sexual abuse by a priest. In that same year and an ocean away, German prelate and theologian Joseph Ratzinger was settling into his new academic post at the University of Regensburg in Germany. Years later, the paths of Clohessy, now the head of the oldest and most active support group of survivors of clergy sexual abuse in the U.S. (SNAP), and Ratzinger, now Pope Benedict XVI, are firmly intertwined.

In his response to a national interview, Clohessy said, "The Church is radically different than every other aspect of our society. It is the world's oldest monarchy. In the United States other secular—or even religious—institutions must respond to a crisis or die. Only five or six bishops have been forced out of office. Four of them stepped aside in Ireland. Otherwise there is not a bishop in the world who drives a smaller car, takes a shorter vacation, does his own laundry, or experiences real consequences for covering up child sex crimes."[1]

Nicholas P. Cafardi, a civil and canon lawyer at Duquesne University School of Law, said the new norms from Cardinal Levada, the prefect of the *Congregation for the Doctrine of the Faith*, were a step forward in the Church's law regarding the sexual abuse of children. The changes were:

1. Victims of sexual abuse by a priest have up to age thirty-eight to report the crime and have it canonically prosecuted.
2. Sexual abuse by clergy of incompetent victims beyond the years of childhood is now considered the same crime as abusing a minor.
3. Acquisition, possession or distribution of child pornography is a canonical crime in and of itself.

In Cafardi's view, these reforms are for the good and apply to the Church in every part of the world. That leaves the Church Universal a few steps behind the position of the Church in the United States. The universal norms announced by Levada, according to Cafardi, do not include the "zero tolerance" policy of the American Church. That policy was adopted by the U.S. bishops at their 2002 meeting and approved by the Apostolic See. The embarrassment of the forced resignation of one of their colleagues, Cardinal Law, as archbishop of Boston caused the U.S. bishops to approve a strict norm, which reads: "The diocesan bishop/eparch shall exercise this power of governance to ensure that any priest or deacon who has committed one act of sexual abuse of a minor . . . shall not continue in active ministry."

The question many of us ask is why Levada, the first U.S. head of the *Congregation for the Doctrine of the Faith*, didn't include "zero tolerance" in his new norms. In April 2002 Pope John Paul, addressing the American cardinals at the Vatican, stated, "People need to know there is no place in the priesthood for those who would harm children."

What should happen to bishops who have broken the Church law (Canon 1389, §2) that states, "A person who, through culpable negligence, illegitimately places or omits an act of ecclesiastical power, ministry or function with harm to another is to be punished with a just penalty."

I've heard of two bishops who are anxious about this canon. They knowingly transferred priests child abusers to other parishes, performing an act that caused harm to another. In each case, the pedophile priest continued his criminal life of abusing children in the new parish. Now we have two people breaking the law, the criminal pedophile priest who should be imprisoned and the bishop who should be punished "with a just penalty."

Who makes sure that the Church's legal system of punishing bishops works? What are we Catholic lay people to do? You read in Chapter XIV that the temple police reported an Australian bishop to the Vatican for suggesting that the Catholic Church discuss the possibility of ordaining women and married men to the priesthood to cope with its shortage of priests. The *Congregation for Bishops* listened to them—and a caring, progressive bishop was fired by Benedict XVI. In contrast to that, you read in Chapter VIII how the Vatican ignored correspondence from six former Legionary seminarians accusing their founder, Father Maciel, of sexually molesting them.

Cafardi gives us the answer: "Levada reaffirms that 'the right, as mandated by the Roman Pontiff to judge . . . bishops belongs to the *Congregation for the Doctrine of the Faith*." Cafardi adds, "It is time for some of those canonical trials of bishops who have reassigned priests with a known history of child sexual abuse to start. Only then will we the laity know that the Church has a legal system that works."[2]

While the norms prescribed for the Universal Church to deal with the priest-pedophile crisis fall below the norms prescribed for the United States, the pope's native country of Germany received criticism from its own journalists. In an article published in the *New York Times* on March 23, 2010, Peter Schneider wrote, "Though Germany is a secular country and Catholics make up only one third of the population, the scandal has engendered a national debate . . . about religious education, about single sex institutions, and, above all, about the role of celibacy in the Catholic Church. . . . The current wave of abuse revelations feels particularly German, because the pope is German. . . . While it is too soon to know for sure how the scandals will affect church membership, rumor has it that the number of resignations by churchgoers in Munich, where the Catholic Church is traditionally strong, has doubled or even tripled in the past month."[3]

Catholics in Bavaria were upset that a pedophile priest, Father Hullermann, was brought to Munich for therapy and then allowed to return to the diocese and work with children. When it became public that he was convicted and sentenced to eighteen-month probation, the diocese suspended him. The question is raised—did Archbishop Ratzinger know it? Or did the *Congregation for the Doctrine of the Faith*, which is responsible for cases of sexual abuse, tell the bishops of Germany, as the apostolic nuncio to Ireland intimated to the bishops of Ireland, to follow a "don't ask, don't tell" policy. Surprisingly, Ratzinger is also critical of German Catholicism, calling it "the richest Church in the world, yet with less influence on society than many poorer Churches have in poorer countries."

Catholicism in Germany faces several challenges. There are areas in Germany with Catholic majorities and others with Protestant majorities. The mobility of modern society means there are increasing numbers of interfaith marriages in which married couples face the problem of not being able to share communion. Because secularization is increasing all over Europe and not just in Germany, the Catholic environments that were exclusive are disintegrating and "Free Churches" are being created, made up of former Catholics and former Lutherans. At the same time, attendance by Catholics at Sunday Mass has dropped from 22 percent in 1990 to 13 percent in 2008. Some left the Catholic Church altogether, as they didn't want to pay the Church tax.[4]

Germany, a secular society, does not have the high percentage of practicing Catholics as either Ireland or the United States. The German Catholic Church is, according to Schneider, "benefiting from the breadth of the sexual abuse scandals. Victims are also coming forward from Protestant institutions, from secular boarding schools and elite academies, from children's homes."[5]

Critics in Germany claim that closed institutions where male educators have charge of male students run the risk of sexual abuse. As I experienced in the all-boys boarding school in Cavan, where priests and male teachers were in charge, sexual abuse took place.

Conservative Catholic bishops in Germany join conservative Catholic bishops in Ireland, blaming the sexualization of society and the craziness of the sixties for the sexual abuse of children by clergy. The only difference is that the Germans cite their own cultural language, *Zeitgeist* (the spirit of the time), as the purported cause of sexual abuse of children by clergy. Schneider disagrees, saying, "The figures available so far show the problem is especially severe in the Catholic Church.

Alois Glück, president of the Central Committee of German Catholics, has urged consideration of the 'Church-specific conditions that favor sexual abuse,' which many take as a call for the Church to reconsider the matter of its priests' celibacy."[6]

The German Catholic Church needs reform just as the Churches in Ireland and the U.S. do. Since Pope Benedict XVI is German and leads the universal Catholic Church, how he addresses the fundamental questions that reform groups in Germany are asking will determine whether the Catholic Church in Germany will survive in its current form. Some of the questions being asked by German reformers include:

- Must a person be chaste to exercise the office of priest?
- Does the condition of mandatory celibacy attract sexually disturbed and pedophile men who see the Catholic Church as a haven to cover up their sexual deviations?
- Can the German Church survive if it has to pay the equivalent of two billion dollars to the victims of pedophile clergy, as the Catholic Church in America has paid? The victims in Germany are now beginning to seek financial reparation.
- How will Pope Benedict XVI repair the damage done to the Church in Germany and the world by the hierarchical cover-up to protect pedophile priests, while ignoring the damage to the child victims?

CHAPTER XVI

Vatican Council II and Cardinal Ratzinger

According to German Church historian Peter Schneider, Joseph Ratzinger was the leading voice of conservatism during his time of service in pre-Vatican II Germany as archbishop of Munich and Freising. Schneider describes Germany as a secular country where Catholics comprise one third of the total population. Recognizing Ratzinger's conservative theological leaning, it is easy to understand why he defended the Church as a perfect institution in no need of renewal to meet modern day demands.[1]

I met then-Cardinal Ratzinger in 1986 during my three-month sabbatical in Rome. My memory is of joining eight other Irish-born priests, who were visiting all of the Vatican Congregations as part of our enlightenment in the Eternal City. Our visit to the *Congregation for the Doctrine of the Faith*, headed by Ratzinger, was an emotional letdown by comparison to concelebrating Mass and meeting with Pope John Paul the day before. Instead of embracing us, the future pope sat behind a desk and lectured us about his Congregation. My psychological training told me that the desk served as an emotional block between Ratzinger and us.

Ratzinger had little or no pastoral experience as a young seminarian growing up in Bavaria or, later, as a fledgling priest in Germany. His early years were spent as a professor of theology at various German universities. As reported previously, bishops with only academic experience and no pastoral experience often seem to find it difficult to deal with interpersonal conflicts and with crises such as the priest-pedophile situation.

Before John Paul II assigned him to oversee the Vatican's worldwide response to the priest-pedophile catastrophe, Ratzinger headed the *Congregation for the Doctrine of the Faith*. At one point, he thrust himself into an episcopal personnel problem that was outside of his assigned authority. Without any recorded invitation, he used his influence with Pope John Paul to block the appointment of the favorite candidate, Father Kurt Krenn, as Archbishop of Vienna. Ratzinger thus cleared the way for the appointment of one of his colleagues at the Congregation, Father Hans Groër, to the position in 1986.[2]

The story of Ratzinger's meddling doesn't end there. According to some knowledgeable priests in the Archdiocese of Vienna, Ratzinger opposed Krenn's appointment to the See of Vienna because Krenn had a doctorate in philosophy rather than theology, which Ratzinger preferred. The priests from Vienna added another black mark to the future pope's lack of good judgment when they announced that it was an "open secret" that Groër, a former Benedictine monk, was a known pedophile. If Ratzinger didn't know this, he should have discovered it while performing a comprehensive review of his candidate.

At the time of the appointment, the worst anyone could say about Krenn was that he was "a loose cannon." One year later, Krenn was appointed bishop of the Diocese of Sankt Polten. Like Groër and Ratzinger, he was conservative. He called renewal-minded Catholics within his diocese "anti-Christs." In 2004 a large cache of child pornography and pictures of other unmentionable behaviors was discovered in the seminary under his jurisdiction. Bishop Krenn tried to minimize the story by calling the behavior "boyish pranks."[3] Public backlash to his statement eventually drove him to resign.

Archbishop Groër was forced to resign in 1995 when a thirty-seven-year-old man claimed that Groër had molested him as a teenager. Later, thirteen other young men joined the original accuser in claiming that Groër had also abused them as teenagers. In response to the situation, Pope John Paul II commented that "Christ faced unjust accusations," and he appointed Groër prior of an Austrian monastery.[4]

The distinguished Professor Ratzinger was well qualified to serve as judge and jury evaluating the orthodoxy of theological writings reported to the *Congregation for the Doctrine of the Faith*. However, having no special training in human sexuality, he lacked insight into dealing with the crisis emerging in the Church worldwide (i.e., pedophile priests and the victims of their abuse). When the crisis emerged in Boston during the episcopacy of Cardinal Bernard Law, the Vatican initially labeled the situation an American problem. The second response was to blame the press for giving front-page headlines to every new story of a Catholic priest molesting a child.

Conservatives like Father Richard Neuhaus, a former Lutheran minister who converted to Catholicism, linked the sex abuse by clergy to American libertinism and lack of faithfulness to celibacy in the American Church. Conservatives argued that, after the liberalizing effects of Vatican II and the gay rights movement, bishops and leaders of religious orders ordained too many gay men and looked the other way when those priests broke their vows of celibacy, either with one another or with youths.[5]

The April 19, 2002, *New York Times* reported that John Paul II had invited all of the American cardinals to Rome to meet with him and Cardinal Ratzinger, the director of the Vatican's doctrinal office. The stated purpose was to discuss the mushrooming problem in the United States. Cardinal J. Francis Stafford, head of the Vatican's Pontifical Council for the Laity, was familiar with the problem. As the former archbishop of Denver, he had issued a handbook of policies for his archdiocese in 1991. He proved to be a great asset to the conference, as he was able "to address the cultural differences between American church leaders and Vatican officials who had struggled to grasp the impact of the scandals and the way they [were] handled."[6]

Cardinal Ratzinger was not fully prepared for the reality of tort law and the financial threat it could pose to Church coffers if the civil courts found the Church hierarchy and Vatican culpable for the sexual abuse crimes by virtue of the cover-ups. The other issue that Cardinal Ratzinger could not understand was the openness with which the majority of the American hierarchy dealt with the crisis, as opposed to the secrecy and denial that had been part of the Vatican culture for centuries.

Cardinal Stafford announced the agenda for the two-day conference, not Cardinal Ratzinger, who was assigned to facilitate the meeting. It included several controversial items: mandatory celibacy, the screening of gay candidates for the priesthood, and the role of women in the church. I imagine that the Vatican was not happy when Cardinal Mahoney of Los Angeles held a far-reaching press conference the day before he departed for Rome. Cardinal Mahoney was reputedly one of the most liberal members of the hierarchy in America, as opposed to Cardinal Ratzinger, the most conservative. Mahoney was not afraid to introduce items not on Stafford's agenda: the ordination of women, optional celibacy for men, a larger role for the laity, more transparent decisions by the hierarchy, and creation of a more humble church.

Cardinal Stafford objected, stating that "the ordination of women was definitely not on the table," and adding, "Rome can't be open to changing the faith . . . we don't have the power to change it even if we'd like to."[7] Ratzinger remained silent on the issue, as he was the one who reportedly put the issue of women's ordination in the untouchable faith category at the request of John Paul II.[8] (There is no Scriptural evidence to back up his decision to deny the priesthood to women.)

Some positives emerged from the pedophile abuse crisis. The Church hierarchy is now forced to examine its disciplines and its practice of secrecy, and it must now consider making changes that are necessary and practical in today's world. Addressing clergy and lay attendees at the Protecting God's Children program at Marquette University in April 2011, Archbishop Diarmuid Martin of Dublin voiced a mantra that the hierarchy of the Catholic world should consider as their motto of the future: "Tell the truth and the truth will set us all free."

Progressive theologians and therapists who have treated sexually abusive priests claim that the causes of the crisis are the Church's lack of candor about sexuality and the strictures of priestly celibacy. The problem arises, they say, when sexually stunted and inexperienced young men are recruited into an institution in which sex is taboo; then incubated in an all-male hot house called a seminary; and, finally, deported into a lonely occupation where a good part of their human contact is with young boys.[9]

What if the mindset of openness and sharing authority recommended by Pope John XXIII and the *Documents of Vatican Council II* had been embraced and implemented? Would we still be in agony over the pain and suffering caused to young people by abusive priests who were shielded from justice by a hierarchy more concerned about protecting the good name of the Church and her priests than protecting her innocent children?

CHAPTER XVII

Four Popes: Who is the Winner?

I feel fortunate to have met two popes during my sabbatical in Rome in 1986. Two days before the meeting with Ratzinger, I concelebrated Mass with Pope John Paul II. Following the liturgy, Pope John Paul met us individually. He was charming and personable. Speaking directly to me, he asked, "Where are you from, Father?"

Tempted to say "Ireland," but not wanting to confuse the poor man, I replied, "Paterson, New Jersey, Holy Father."

He replied almost immediately, "Is that near Boston?"

Not wanting to disappoint him, I replied, "Yes, Holy Father."

In the *New York Times* on April 12, 2010, Ross Douthat wrote, "The world didn't always agree with John Paul II, but it always seemed to love him. Handsome and charismatic, with an actor's flair and a statesman's confidence, he transformed the papacy from an Italian anachronism into a globe-trotting phenomenon."[1]

The comparison between the two men was dramatic. John Paul would score high as an extrovert on the *Myers Briggs Personality Scale*, a standard test to measure how people see the world and make decisions. His successor, Benedict XVI, would score in the opposite direction as an introvert. Cardinal Ratzinger, as I reported in an earlier chapter, did not get up from his chair to greet us. He simply gave us a lecture on what functions his Congregation serves in the overall administration of the Church.

In his article, Ross Douthat commented on the personality of the new pope and compared him with John Paul: "The former Joseph Ratzinger was always going to be a harder pontiff for the world to love: more introverted than his predecessor, less political and peripatetic, with the crags and wrinkles of a sinister great, great uncle."[2]

While John Paul loved to travel and interact with presidents and rock stars, Benedict was more comfortable "minding the store," that is, the Vatican. Living up to his nickname "God's Rottweiler," he jostled with liberals like the Swiss theologian Hans Kung and liberation theologians from South America, such as the Brazilian priest Leonardo Boff.

Although Benedict's bookish, defensive attitude and his lack of public relation skills inhibited him from dealing with the priest-pedophile crisis with transparency and candor, he was a better administrator than John Paul, who is already condemned to history as a poor delegator and a woeful judge of character. John Paul misjudged Father Marcial Maciel Degollado, founder of the *Legion of Christ*. Maciel raised millions of dollars from wealthy families in the United States, Spain, and Mexico and from his own Legion centers in those countries. He used these millions to ingratiate himself to the major Church officials in Rome, funneling the money to pivotal figures in the papal household of John Paul, who was deceived by Maciel.

The list of bribed officials close to the Pope was impressive. Chief among them were Cardinal Sodano, Vatican secretary of state from 1996 to 2006, now dean of the College of Cardinals; Cardinal Eduardo Somalo, prefect of the *Congregation of Consecrated Life and Apostolic Life*; and Monsignor Stanislaus Dziwiscz, the Polish secretary and John Paul's aide, whom I also met in Rome and whose inclusion is still a surprise to me. Recently, when a journalist from the *National Catholic Reporter* called on now-Cardinal Dziwiscz in his native Poland for an interview regarding this subject, his secretary replied, "The cardinal does not have time for such an interview."[3] The question remains, where did the bags of money go?

To give Benedict his due, he was suspicious of Maciel from the outset and was the first to see through his methods of operation. After giving a theology lecture to the Legion of Christ seminarians in Rome when he was prefect of the *Congregation*, he refused to accept an envelope full of money from Maciel.

John Paul was not as fortunate. Against the advice of his advisors, he entrusted the Legion with the administration of the Jerusalem Notre Dame Center, a well-known education and conference establishment in the heart of the Holy City. The Center's inauguration ceremony was held at the Vatican in 2004.

God's Rottweiler was not impressed. The following week he authorized an investigation of Maciel, who, as a result, was sent into spiritual exile to atone for his sins and prepare to meet his Creator at death. Years later on July 9, 2010, the Associated Press reported that, after an eight-month investigation of the order, Pope Benedict had named a senior Vatican official to run the scandal-plagued Legion of Christ. This action would not have taken place under John Paul's watch.

*   *   *

John Paul and Benedict were preceded by two pontiffs with dramatically different profiles. The aging Pope John XXIII was an extrovert like John Paul, while Paul VI was not as introverted as Benedict. To give Paul his due, he had big shoes to fill in succeeding Pope John XXIII. Before he assumed the role of Pontiff and Vicar of Christ in 1963, he served in the Vatican State Department for thirty-two years, which denied him the more typical pastoral experience of ministering to individuals, couples and families at the parish level.

Paul VI was born into a highly respected aristocratic family on September 26, 1897. His father was a lawyer and a member of the Italian parliament. His mother, Guidetta Alghisi, was from a family of rural nobility. While in the State Department, Giovanni Battista Enrico Antonio Maria Montini (Paul VI's christened name) was one of Pope Pius XII's most influential co-workers. Pius appointed him Archbishop of Milan, the largest diocese in Italy. This position automatically made him secretary of the National Bishops Conference, giving him influence over the entire Italian Catholic population at age 57. Pope John XXIII elevated him to the College of Cardinals in 1958. Following the death of the popular Pope John, Montini stood out as the favored successor.

In contrast to other popes, Paul VI was a pure intellectual and saw himself as a humble servant ministering to suffering humanity and demanding sacrifices from the rich in Europe and the United States in favor of the poor in the Third World. When he chose the name Paul for his pontificate, he was obviously imitating the great apostle St. Paul, with the goal of following in his footsteps by spreading the Gospel of Jesus Christ to every corner of the world.

Vatican Council II was automatically closed with the death of Pope John on June 3, 1963. Paul VI immediately reopened it, with a new direction and a revised purpose. At the beginning of his term, he appeared to be following the mindset of his predecessor in initiating a dialogue with the world at large, including with other Christian Churches, Muslims, Hindus, Buddhists, and even atheists.

Nobody was excluded from his vision. He used his acclaimed intellect to implement many of the changes mandated by the Council Fathers. This meant walking the narrow line between the ultra-conservative *Curia*, conservative cardinals and bishops on the one side and the progressive clergy and laity on the other. This monumental task for Paul demanded the use of all his diplomatic skills, the entire process taking place during the turbulent sixties. Some historians claim that the magnitude and depth of Paul VI's reforms exceeded all the reforms of his predecessors and successors to date.

Paul VI was deeply respected in Ireland, primarily because of his devotion to Mary the Mother of God. He accepted every invitation to speak at Marian congresses and participated in forums dedicated to studying Mary's role in the modern world. During the second half of the Vatican Council he gave Mary the new title "Mother of the Church."

He became the first pope to visit all six continents, earning the designation of "The Pilgrim Pope." Older readers will remember his first visit to the United States in 1965. What an extraordinary moment it was to witness Christ's Vicar on earth addressing the United Nations and pleading for peace. He exhorted, "No more war, never again war. It is peace that must guide the destinies of people and of all mankind."[4]

Like his predecessor Pius XII, Paul emphasized dialogue among all nations. During his pontificate, the Vatican doubled the number of its foreign embassies. He was the primary mover in developing a clear understanding of the difference between State power and Church authority. The pastoral constitution *Gaudium et Spes* stated clearly that the Catholic Church was not bound by any form of government and yet was willing to conform to all forms of government.

It is not clear when Pope Paul moved from following the liberal footsteps of his predecessor Pope John, but it became evident once he began to take control of the Council. He dictated to the Council Fathers what to do and how to address several issues on the Council's agenda. This was a very different approach from the one used by Pope John, and some of the Council Fathers accused him of meddling in the affairs of the Council. The American bishops pushed for a speedy resolution to the issue of religious freedom, but Pope Paul insisted that this item be included with related texts on Ecumenism. He asked the Council Fathers not to repeat or create any new documents on the nature of the Church, but to explain in simple terms how the Church saw itself and its mission to the modern world.

During the period between the third and fourth sessions of the Council, while the cardinals and bishops were away from the Vatican, Pope Paul announced reforms in the areas of the *Roman Curia* and revision of Canon Law, as well as regulations for interfaith marriages and birth control.

Many progressive cardinals, bishops and *periti* were upset that he refused to let them discuss possible reforms regarding married couples' use of contraceptives to control pregnancies. As reported in a previous chapter, Pope Paul continued John XXIII's commission of theologians, and he added married couples. When they reported back to him, he ignored the majority opinion submitted by his own commission on the grounds that the commission used "certain approaches and criteria for a solution to this question, which were at variance with the moral doctrine on marriage consistently taught by the Church *Magisterium*."

When *Humanae Vitae* was published, Pope Paul VI wrote: "*We base Our words on the first principles of a human and Christian doctrine of marriage when We are obliged once more to declare that the direct interruption of the generative process already begun* [which included a condemnation of abortion and sterilization] *and likewise any action which either before, at the moment of, or after sexual intercourse is specifically intended to prevent procreation, whether as an end or as a means to an end, are to be absolutely excluded as lawful means for regulating the number of children."*

Score a win for the *Curia* and the conservative hierarchy and a loss for progressive clergy, theologians and married lay couples.

CHAPTER XVIII

Roncalli: Student, Seminarian and Priest

Older baseball fans will recall the fierce rivalry between the New York Giants and the Brooklyn Dodgers, just as many of we "senior" Catholics remember the unspoken rivalry between conservative and liberal theologians over the past fifty-plus years. Giant fans still talk about the so-called "shot heard around the world" when Bobby Thompson, the Giant slugger, hit a three-run homer into the lower deck on October 3, 1951, giving the Giants a 5 to 4 pennant win over their rivals, the Dodgers.

Likewise, progressive Catholics remember with similar joy the aging, so-called stop-gap Pope John XXIII, in words heard around the world, making the stunning announcement that he was calling an ecumenical council. "It is time to open up the windows of the Church and let in some fresh air," he proclaimed on January 25, 1959, less than three months after his election as pope in October 1958.

Angelo Roncalli had something else in common with Bobby Thompson. They were both humble citizens who enjoyed playing the game of life, with no desire to seek the limelight. As history has already recorded, they will both be remembered with affection and admiration.

Unlike his successor Paul VI, John XXIII was the son of peasants. He once announced in Venice, "We were poor but happy. We did not realize we lacked anything and in truth we didn't. Ours was a dignified and happy poverty."[1]

In 1959 Zsolt Aradi, Monsignor James I. Tucek, and James C. O'Neill published a detailed biography based on their contacts with the pope's relatives, friends and associates. They wrote, "The Roncalli family's domestic life was a happy one, because it was based on peace and obedience: peace between members of the family, obedience of the children to their parents, and both parents' and children's obedience to God."[2]

Angelo Roncalli walked the three miles to school along with the other peasant children. He was not an outstanding student. To help him do better educationally, his dad enrolled him at age nine in the Episcopal High School at Celano. He took a piece of polenta in his school bag for lunch, and to save his shoes he walked barefoot to school, as long as the weather permitted. Two years later he entered the seminary five miles away in Bergamo.

This transfer opened up new windows to the world for young Angelo. The seminary taught many students, not only prospective priests. The curriculum was general and included courses in Latin, Greek, Italian, world history, mathematics, geography, physics, chemistry and world literature. Angelo became a brilliant student. His biographers note that his "personality was well balanced, his interests proportionally divided, with a decisive inclination towards history. He was a healthy young man, liked equally by professors and fellow students."[3]

His father's decision to transfer Angelo to Episcopal High School led, fortuitously, to his acceptance at the respected seminary in Bergamo. Bergamo was already a historical city and the center of Italian Catholicism. Angelo blossomed educationally and socially. He was very much influenced by the progressive social activity in the Diocese of Bergamo. Like many seminarians, he had models to emulate, both in the priesthood and among the faculty. Monsignor Radini-Tedeschi was an outstanding organizer of Catholic Action, while Professor Nicolo Rezzara was secretary general of the most progressive social institution of the Italian Catholics, the *Unione Popolare Ecanomico Sociale*. These men were the two most influential people in Angelo's life during his formative years in the seminary.

Angelo's formal journey toward the priesthood accelerated when he received the Order of Tonsure at the very young age of 14. In 1900

Angelo was sent to the Roman Seminary on a scholarship from the Cerasoli Foundation. The Church had several theological seminaries in Italy, but the Roman Seminary was regarded as one of the most important pontifical institutions for the education of priests. Only those with exceptional qualities, including a higher potential for leadership, received this opportunity.

Inspired by his mentors and by the spiritual and intellectual world he experienced at Bergamo, he was ready to focus on studying Canon Law and history, particularly the history of religions and of the Catholic Church. The young Angelo arrived in Rome right in the middle of the Holy Year 1900 when pilgrims from all continents and races were converging on Rome to receive the Apostolic Blessing from the ninety-year-old pontiff Pope Leo XIII.

The avalanche of pilgrims didn't distract the studious Angelo, who was by this time inspired by the writings of St. Philip Neri (1515-1595), the Blessed Cesare Cardinal Baroni (1538-1607) and St. Frances De Sales (1567-1622). In 1900 his studies were interrupted when he volunteered, like many of his fellow seminarians, for military service. Being a healthy, solidly built twenty-year-old, he joined the infantry, a good choice for a boy who had walked several miles back and forth to school. He was a fine soldier, physically strong, with common sense and an aptitude for comradeship.

He was ordained a priest on August 10, 1904, and, the next day, celebrated his first Mass at the altar in the grotto of St. Peter's, which, tradition has it, is next to St. Peter's tomb. Like most newly ordained priests, he returned to the village of Sotto il Monte and, amidst his family and villagers, offered Mass on August 15. His entire family was there. I can personally identify with the awe and respect that the newly ordained Father Roncalli received on that memorable day. He was still one of them, and yet he was different. The older priests, who participated that day, knew that their local boy, now a newly ordained priest, was meant for an even higher calling.

After a summer at home he returned to the seminary in Rome to complete his studies for a doctorate in theology and to initiate the journey toward a doctorate in Canon Law. His primary goal was to become a parish priest like the older priests who participated in his first

Mass in his home village. This was not going to happen, as the newly appointed bishop of Bergamo, Bishop Radini-Tedeschi, chose the one-year-ordained Father Roncalli to be his secretary. This sudden and unexpected appointment moved the young priest into the mainstream of national and international Catholicism.

Bishop Radini-Tedeschi's family background was different than Angelo's. He came from a well-to-do Piacenza family with many nuns and priests. Yet, they had very much in common. Both were selected by their superiors very early in their priesthood to serve in important ecclesiastical positions. Radini-Tedeschi was only thirty-three years old when called by Pope Leo XIII to serve in the Secretariat of State, while Angelo was just twenty-four years old when he was appointed the bishop's secretary. Both of these men had superior people skills and put service to people above any personal ambition. They each possessed a belief in the Church and in its mission to the world and, above all, a loyal obedience to the Holy Father the Pope.

Even though Father Roncalli never worked closely with Pope Leo XIII, much of what was achieved or pursued during the papacy of Pope Leo was a foretaste of what would happen later during the papacy of John XXIII. While still a seminarian in Rome from 1900 to his ordination in 1904, Angelo witnessed this influential pontiff restoring the power of the papacy. Aradi, Tucek and O'Neill report, "This great Pope enjoyed universal prestige before the people, their governments, both the rulers of Catholic and non-Catholic countries."[4] He gained the respect of the German civil authorities and encouraged Anglicans and Catholics to resume talks about reunification. He also made various attempts to bridge the gap between the Eastern Orthodox Church and Rome.

Pope Leo kept an open mind and built a mature relationship with France in spite of its anti-religious laws and the anti-clerical temperament of the government. He wholeheartedly agreed with the social ideas of the progressive workers of Italy, but he was against their participation in national politics. The young Roncalli was not involved in these "political" problems of the Holy See. However, he would have been conscious of all that was happening at the Vatican while he studied theology and Church history.

Looking back now, it was unfortunate that this influential pope died in 1903, one year before the young Roncalli's ordination to the priesthood. However, Leo XIII's influence on the seminarian Roncalli took root and affected his ministry and his own spiritual journey toward the papacy.

During their time together, Bishop Radini-Tedeschi and Father Roncalli became known as excellent preachers. Father Roncalli learned the importance of good liturgical celebrations as he observed his bishop preside at ceremonies. Both had a deep devotion to Mary, the Mother of Jesus. Roncalli accompanied his bishop five times on pilgrimages to Our Lady's Shrine in Lourdes, France. He admired Radini as both an administrator and a spiritual leader, and he learned the elements of real leadership from his boss. Roncalli's biographers describe his innate ability to lead using his own words: "To know what one wants to do, if one has the responsibility of command, so that people may follow him; to express firmness of intent in a calm, non-dictatorial way."[5]

In addition to serving as secretary to the bishop, at the age of twenty-three Roncalli also taught Church history and apologetics at the seminary. The students loved his enthusiasm and conviction as he taught the course, spiked with colorful anecdotes from his family and from his days in Rome. He didn't, however, allow his duties as a professor or researcher of Church history to take away from his duties as secretary to the bishop. Father Roncalli was very sad when Bishop Radini died on August 22, 1914. The bishop was only fifty-seven years old. This was in contrast to Pope Pius X, who had died two days earlier at the age of seventy-nine.

To demonstrate his love and respect for Radini, Roncalli wrote two biographies about him over the next several years. He was not going to have too many free years to mourn the loss of his friend and spiritual mentor. He was called up the following year in 1915 to serve in the Italian army as a chaplain ministering to the sick and dying soldiers of the First World War.

In his 1916 biography of Radini, Roncalli wrote: "These pages were written while in Europe, as the war went on, the horrible war that caused so much bloodshed and tears. I have written these lines and worked on this book not in the sweet quietness of the life of studies but amidst the most varied occupations following the teachings and example of Monsignor Radini . . . first for several months as a simple soldier, then as a non-commissioned officer of the lowest rank, and finally more directly as a priest."[6]

CHAPTER XIX

Roncalli: Soldier to Archbishop and Diplomat

Following the death of Pope Pius X, the way in which the cardinals chose his successor in the conclave in Rome demonstrates how politics may affect the selection of a pope. Benedict XV was the unexpected choice. This frail and sensitive aristocrat was chosen primarily because he opposed the war and didn't favor either side in the conflict that became known as the Great War of 1914-1918. In fact, he spent many hours trying first to prevent the war, then trying to persuade Kaiser Wilhelm II, king of Prussia and emperor of Germany, and the Western Allies to end it. One can speculate whether, if Angelo Roncalli had been born fifty or sixty years earlier and was chosen Pope John XXIII at that time, rather than the frail Pope Benedict XV, would the war ever have happened?

The war ended in November 1918, and reconstruction of human lives and bombed-out buildings began. Father Roncalli, serving as army chaplain, was discharged from military service and, to no one's surprise, dedicated himself to work among the many students who had returned wounded from the war. In 1919 he created a "Student House," a home away from home, a clubhouse, for high school students. He later returned to the seminary to teach.[1]

Roncalli slowly and steadily climbed the ecclesiastical ladder. The new bishop of Bergamo, Bishop Marelli, was concerned about the psychological well-being of the seminarians, some experiencing post-traumatic stress, others threatened by the growth of communism in Italy as the workers marched under the red flag. The bishop, anxious to place the seminarians in strong hands, appointed Roncalli spiritual director of the seminary. Roncalli knew how to deal with seminarians. He gained their confidence in a very short time, allowing them to feel safe under his caring guidance.

This honeymoon was not going to last. News of Roncalli's talents reached Rome. He was just forty years old when he received a call from the Vatican. Pope Benedict XV was calling him to Rome to serve as an official of the *Sacred Congregation for the Propagation of the Faith*. This Congregation was in disarray following the war because the simultaneous presence of both Catholic and Protestant missionaries had created a contradiction. After being taught Christ's love and the superiority of the Christian faith, these colonial natives were sent to fight against other Christian people.

Pope Benedict was conscious of Roncalli's outstanding organizational skills and knew he was grounded in sound spiritual, political and intellectual foundations. It was no secret that Pope Benedict was a close friend of the late Bishop Radini-Tedeschi. Benedict was also aware of Roncalli's friendship with Radini-Tedeschi, which influenced his decision to call Roncalli back to Rome. He felt confident that Roncalli could and would straighten out the mess.[2]

Benedict XV was not around to witness Roncalli's success, as he died a few months later. His successor, Achille Ratti, had been elevated to cardinal by Benedict a few months before his death. Church skeptics and critics would point out that even a dying pope was capable of manipulating the cardinals in conclave to pick a like-minded thinker as his successor. The new pope chose the name Pius XI and acted quickly to make certain that Roncalli remained as healer of the congregation he now served. He promoted Roncalli to prothonotary apostolic, which meant that he was given the title of Monsignor. Roncalli had not yet reached his forty-first birthday. He became a member of the Supreme Council and president of the national branch of the Congregation that covered all of Italy. His job was to ensure that those missionaries going abroad to spread the Gospel had an adequate supply of books, portable altars, medical supplies, and means of transportation.

As with many people in leadership positions who follow the maxim "If you want a job done and done well, you give it to a busy person," in 1925 the pope also appointed Roncalli to the Central Committee for the Holy Year. Roncalli was in charge of creating an exhibition that would demonstrate the work of missionaries by using scenes from the countries in which they served. Scenes of life in Africa, Australia, Latin America, and elsewhere were illustrated with life-size wax figures dressed in the native clothing of the region.

This appointment for the Holy Year served as a novitiate for his first international assignment, which happened later that year. Cynics will say that Roncalli was always lucky to be in the right place at the right time when an ecclesiastical leader was needed. Others may say that being well connected catapulted his career to stardom. The truth is that he had a natural capacity for leadership and learned the necessary elements of real leadership from his mentors and from his research into the lives of St. Philip Neri and St. Charles Borromeo (1538-1584).

Following the "good luck" theory, and without being too cynical, it seems that Roncalli again soon found himself in the right place at the right time. The apostolic administrator of the Latin Rite Catholics in Bulgaria died, leaving a plethora of unresolved problems among the fifty thousand Catholics living there in the midst of a major population of the Eastern Orthodox Church. The problems were connected and complicated, requiring Pope Pius XI to send an apostolic visitor to Sofia, Bulgaria, to investigate and then report back to the Vatican with suggested solutions.

Pope Pius made up his mind quickly and appointed Roncalli the Apostolic Visitor to Bulgaria. The tradition at that time was that any representative of the Holy See, whether they were a visitor or full-fledged nuncio, always had the rank of archbishop. It didn't matter that Roncalli was just twenty years ordained; he was consecrated with all the pomp and circumstance on March 19, 1925, in Rome's San Carlo al Corso Church, which was named after one of the new archbishop's favorite saints, St. Charles Borromeo. The Vatican's semi-official newspaper *L'Osservatore Romano* announced the appointment, pointing out that Archbishop Roncalli was a priest imbued with sound piety, intelligence, formidable learning, good judgment, harmonious character and sense of balance.[3]

Before he set off for Sophia he visited his family in the village of Sotto il Monte. His biographers recall how he enjoyed being with his own people. His mother was sixty-eight and his father seventy-one. His married siblings still lived in the same house. Angelo shared their life and walked humbly among the folks in the village. He ate their simple meals and drank their homemade wine; he laughed and played with the children.

His biographers don't say how his parents felt when he packed his bags and left Milan on the Simplon-Orient-Express traveling to Sophia. They may have been like my parents in August 1960 when I boarded the Aer Lingus flight at the Dublin airport to New York, probably proud of their son but sad that God was calling him to leave his homeland and do His will in a foreign land.

The new archbishop traveled with his secretary, a Benedictine monk, who was knowledgeable about all the problems related to the Oriental Church. They arrived in the capital of Bulgaria on April 25, 1925. It would be nice to report that the new archbishop was given a warm welcome at his new mission in the Byzantine world, but Macedonian terrorists had just assassinated the prime minister of the Balkan kingdom. The *Catholic Weekly* wrote, "At the time of [the new patriarch's] arrival, one could smell the smoke . . . a smoke that spread over the whole country." Nine days earlier, a time bomb had exploded in the Orthodox Cathedral Svate Nedelja during the prime minister's funeral, killing 123 people, while King Boris escaped.

Fortunately, there was no instant communication back home to the Roncalli family in their little village. He was destined to spend twenty years in the troubled lands of Bulgaria and Turkey, knowing from the beginning that his many talents as a healer and as the pope's representative would be challenged in these war-torn and violent communities.

The question arises, why did Pope Pius XI send an apostolic visitor to a country as troubled as Bulgaria? And why did he authorize it at this time? The aim of the Holy Father was clear. Bulgaria was a Catholic nation with a deep religious faith. It was very poor and needed help in building churches and institutions to meet the needs of their people. Archbishop Roncalli had the personality and the training to meet all of their needs. In addressing a group of Bulgarian Catholics who visited

Pope Pius at the Vatican, he told them, "I have sent you my envoy to represent my person. He will have my ears that I should hear you, my lips that I should talk to you and my heart that you should feel how much I love you."

Roncalli possessed two characteristics not always present in Vatican diplomats. He was not full of himself, expecting both civil and Church authorities to be subservient as if he was a full-fledged representative of the Holy See. Secondly, he chose to follow his heart, using his Italian peasant common sense and priestly training.

He began his ministry in Sophia by visiting the hundreds of wounded who filled the hospitals after the war. No distinction was made between Catholics or Orthodox. Everybody received his priestly blessing. The Orthodox priests were amazed at his humility and kindness, with several of them stating that their own authorities would not have cared for the wounded with as much love as he. The news spread over the country. Several representatives of the Bulgarian government and diplomatic corps, as well as representatives of all Christian faiths, attended Roncalli's inaugural speech, a sermon in the Catholic cathedral of Sophia. Years later, when, as Patriarch of Venice, he was asked about this success in Bulgaria, he simply said he never considered himself primarily a diplomat or teacher, but simply a priest. He repeated this same answer when he became pope.[4]

CHAPTER XX

Roncalli: Archbishop to Cardinal

Pope Pius XI died in 1939. By this time Roncalli had been transferred to Istanbul as the newly appointed apostolic delegate to both Turkey and Greece. His additional responsibility included taking care of the tiny Catholic flock. Most Christians were of the Orthodox faith, which didn't come under the jurisdiction of the pope and the *Curia*. Although Roncalli made some inroads to reuniting the Orthodox Christians with the Vatican, he was disappointed that unification did not take place before the death of his favorite pope. With a saddened heart, he offered a solemn Requiem Mass for the late Holy Father in the Holy Ghost Basilica of Istanbul. As a demonstration of the Turkish Government's acceptance and admiration for Archbishop Roncalli, several members of the diplomatic corps and Turkish government officials attended the service.

During the homily Archbishop Roncalli recalled the personality of the deceased pope and revealed as much as he was at liberty to share with the congregation about the pope's desire for Christian Unity when he said, "The limits which the circumstances impose on me advise me not to lift here before you the most precious veil of secrecy." Unable to reveal entirely all he knew about the desires and instructions of the late pope with regard to the unity of all Christians, he added, "Time veils and unveils everything. . . . The day will come, perhaps it is still far away, when the vision of Christ of one shepherd and one flock will become the lovely reality of heaven and earth. In that day the particular merits of Pius XI will become resplendent in their evidence."[1]

Roncalli spent from 1925 to 1945 in Turkey. During the second decade there, he organized communication between prisoners of war of all nations with their relatives, and, as well, found missing persons and refugees who were scattered all over the world. Because of his engaging personality, he was able to get information about prisoners of war (POWs) and people in concentration camps whom even the International Red Cross was unable to trace. Roncalli was instrumental in aiding Jewish refugees who fled Nazi Germany and helping them reach Palestine.

Roncalli's location in Turkey and the Vatican's neutral position on the war gave him a unique position with both friend and foe, all of whom approached him with ideas and requests for help and information. When the war was over, Franz von Papen, the German ambassador to Turkey, asked Roncalli to persuade the Vatican to convince the Allies that they should make a distinction between the German people and the Third Reich. Later, in his memoir, von Papen wrote, "At my request [Roncalli] forwarded my pleas to the Vatican that the Allies should realize the difference between the Hitler regime and the German people."[2] Roncalli served as a conduit of communication between the Orthodox Church and the Vatican and, later, between the Orthodox Church and the British Government, which occupied Greece at the time.

Historians tell us that the atmosphere for initiating Christian Unity was very favorable after the war. Leaders of different Christian faiths believed that peace could not be secured without the practical application of Christian principles in international relations and in the relationship of Christian churches among themselves. Roncalli was troubled that during his twenty years as apostolic delegate in the Byzantine world he had been unable to achieve Christian Unity.

Alden Hatch, author of *A Man Named John: The Life of Pope John XXIII*, gives some insights as to why Apostolic Delegate Roncalli, in spite of his renowned diplomatic skills, was not more successful in persuading the Orthodox Christians to rejoin Roman Catholicism. He wrote, "The Orthodox Church was the official Church of Bulgaria and was proud of its power and independence from Rome. Although many Orthodox

Bulgarians would have liked to rejoin their Mother Church, a majority of them and almost all the higher clergy, were violently against it. They suspected the Holy See of devious machinations to produce this result and watched every move the Archbishop made with hostile eyes. . . . This man (Roncalli) could not conspire to, nor would attempt to, bring them back to the fold against their wills."[3]

On the other side of the spectrum, the leader of the Orthodox Church held Roncalli in high respect, as was evident in Hatch's report on the occasion of Roncalli's appointment as the permanent apostolic delegate to Bulgaria. He wrote, "King Boris alone could not have permitted this advancement if he had not had the consent of the (Orthodox) Exarchate.[4]

In December 1944 a ciphered telegram arrived from Rome addressed to the apostolic delegate. Roncalli had a lot of intelligence, but he was not trained in decoding telegrams. After a few hours, his secretary returned to the office and decoded the telegram, which contained the message that the pope had appointed Roncalli as papal nuncio to Paris and that he was to proceed to Rome at once. With typical humor and humility he responded, "I think they have lost their minds in Rome."

He asked his good friend Monsignor Tardini whether it was possible the telegram was sent in error. Tardini's jibe in return caused both of them to have a good laugh. "Angelo, nobody that I know of expected this to ever happen."[5]

The new nuncio arrived in Paris on December 31, 1944, and immediately presented his credentials. The following day he offered the traditional New Years greetings to General Charles DeGaulle. Roncalli had the reputation of always being been able to say the right thing and in the right spirit. He told DeGaulle, "Thanks to your political foresight and to your energy, this beloved country has once more found her liberty and faith in her destiny."[6]

Cynics will say that the nuncio was exaggerating, as the France he was sent to in 1944 was no longer known for its spiritual and intellectual greatness. As a result of two wars, the nation was torn asunder by both political and ideological conflicts. From a religious viewpoint, the split within France was even deeper. The Catholics were divided in two camps: right-wing extremists versus the high percentage of left-leaning, anticlerical critics and others possessing socialist and communist ideologies. The head of state, Marshall Petain, a believing and practicing Catholic, used his power to abolish some of the anti-church and anti-clerical laws. One of the laws was that priests were drafted into the army—not to serve as chaplains, but as soldiers.

Today's historians agree that Roncalli was entrusted with a very difficult task by the Holy See when they appointed him papal nuncio to Paris. The apostolic delegate at that time, Monsignor Giacomo Testa, reported, "He arrived in Paris at a very critical moment and had immediately to face a delicate situation. All sorts of passions and hatreds were unleashed in France; a wind that concealed the germs of revolution blew over the country. Roncalli's smiling goodness, his calm, his patience, his firmness, his ability to overcome difficulties and obstacles saved the Church and France from real catastrophe. . . . He navigated between rocks and went ahead with prudence."[7]

The most prominent conflict involved General DeGaulle's accusation that the bishops of France were collaborating with the Vichy Regime, which favored making peace with Hitler. DeGaulle demanded that Roncalli remove thirty-three bishops. By the force of his personality, Roncalli forced DeGaulle to allow an adequate investigation of the accusations. The government consented, and the investigation lasted one year. At the conclusion, only three bishops resigned.

In contrast to some of his predecessors, Roncalli's line of conduct was simple and precise. The Church in its ministry obeyed Rome and remained apart from the temporal and political affairs of their host country. It was this philosophy that reestablished equilibrium between Church and State. His predecessors looked upon the government as an adversary. He was more tolerant of government officials and would frequently say, "In my case it is different. I feel like I am among friends."[8] This was a typical Roncalli expression, showing his character and his successful method of dealing with politicians.

Roncalli traveled widely in France, as he had in Bulgaria, Turkey, and Greece. He visited all but two of the eighty-seven dioceses of France. Whether he was involved in civic or Church conflict, his personality became the main factor of reconciliation. His usual schedule included visiting one diocese per month. He studied the history of each area and arranged visits with local civic leaders on the occasion of those visits. People were drawn to his magnetic personality.

By 1951 he was the most beloved diplomat in France, well known to government officials, clergy and the French people, both Catholic and non-Catholic. Through all the adulation and prominence as a diplomat of the Holy See, he remained a priest who praised Jesus Christ, Savior of mankind and Son of God. Aradi, Tucek and O'Neill report on the times of conflict between Worker-Priests and the French authority when Edouard Heriot, a militant French anti-clerical who was profoundly attracted by Roncalli's personality, made the bitter remark, "If all the priests were like Roncalli, we would have no trouble with the Catholic Church."[9]

In December 1952 Roncalli received news from Pope Pius XII that any ambitious cleric would have been very pleased to hear: Pope Pius was going to elevate Roncalli to the cardinalate. This was not how Roncalli received the news. He would not disrespect the Holy Father by refusing; instead he accepted in the spirit of his motto *Obedientia et Pax* (Obedience and Peace). When one of his cardinal colleagues visited him to wish Roncalli *Tanti Auguri* (Congratulations), he found Roncalli sitting quietly and sadly reading his Divine Office. When asked about it, Roncalli replied, "Now I have to leave Paris, leave France and all this is painful for me. I'm not happy at the thought of spending the rest of my life among Roman paperwork in the offices of the Congregations."[10] The French Republic gave him a memorable going-away celebration. His faithful assistant Monsignor Giacomo Testa brought the cardinal's biretta to the lavish ceremony on January 15, 1953. The celebration was held at the Elysee, the residence of the president of the Republic of France.

President Vincent Auriol, in an ecumenical gesture, placed the red biretta on Roncalli's head in the presence of two emissaries from Rome; the former French prime minister Rene Viviani, who was Jewish; and the Canadian ambassador, who was a Calvinist. President Auriol, a longtime socialist and former Marxist, spoke for all of France when he addressed Roncalli, saying: "The French government was profoundly touched by your constant cordiality and by your concern for peace in our country according to the noble and paternal teachings of the supreme head of the Church. We are profoundly appreciative of all your generous initiatives for peace. . . . Your messages will remain for all of us examples of wisdom, finesse and friendship. The displeasure that we feel because of your departure is sweetened by the joy of knowing that there will be among the Princes of the Church one who is so profoundly *au courant* about French affairs and is a sincere and firm friend."[11]

While the Catholic world celebrated and embraced the rising star Cardinal Angelo Roncalli, American sports enthusiasts celebrated another son of sharecropper parents making news in America's favorite sport of baseball. Jackie Roosevelt Robinson broke the color barrier by becoming the first black player to be accepted into the all-white United States Major League in 1947. The Brooklyn Dodgers became his home, and later that year he won the title of Rookie of the Year. Two years later this rising star was voted the National League's most valuable player.

Jackie's life and legacy will be remembered not only as an historical event in baseball lore but also as an important step in American democracy. Likewise, Cardinal Roncalli, another man of humble origins, was destined to change the Catholic world by his vision, leadership and humility to serve the world primarily as a priest. As Roncalli said, "In beholding your Patriarch, seek the priest, the minister of grace and nothing else."

CHAPTER XXI

Roncalli: Cardinal to Pope

The year was 1953. Who would be that year's World Series Champions? In a classic rematch of the previous year's World Series, "The Bronx Bombers," as the Yankees were called, were challenged by their cross-town rivals "The Bums from Brooklyn," the nickname for the Brooklyn Dodgers. The Yankees were determined to retain the crown, while the Dodgers were ready for revenge. Baseball fans still talked about Bobby Thompson's 1951 so-called "Shot heard around the World." The heroes of the 1953 series were Yankee sluggers Mickey Mantle and Billy Martin, who both hit home runs. Mickey's was a grand slam that brought in four runs.

In that same year, Angelo Roncalli, the newly elevated Cardinal was as lucky as a Bronx Bomber. He feared being assigned to what he envisioned as the boring paperwork of the *Curia* offices or a Congregation at the Vatican. He knew and admired Patriarch of Venice Carlo Agostini, and he regretted that Agostini didn't live to receive his cardinal's red hat with Roncalli on January 12, 1953. The silver lining of the tragedy was that he, Cardinal Roncalli, was named by Pius XII to replace Agostini as the new Patriarch of Venice. This appointment helped relieve the pain Roncalli felt in leaving Paris.

By 1953 Roncalli's reputation as a Church leader, a man of God and peacemaker, had spread all over the Catholic world. On March 15, 2003, the new patriarch made a triumphant entry into the "City of Canals."

While most of us are thinking of retiring at Roncalli's age of seventy-one, this was the last thing on Roncalli's mind as he greeted all the boats and gondolas of Venice that turned out to meet their new spiritual leader. This proud city, which once dominated the seas, decorated all the boats and gondolas with flowers, while the gold insignias of churches floated down the canal, preceding the launch on which the patriarch rode. With a big smile he blessed all the people lining the edges of the canal and the bridges.

Arriving at St. Mark's Square with his entourage of bishops and clergy, the patriarch entered the Basilica, while the choir intoned the solemn hymn of thanksgiving *Te Deum.* In his usual transparent and simple manner he said, "*Ecce homo, ecce sacerdos, ecce pastor* (Behold the man, behold the priest, behold the pastor.) I wish to speak to you with the greatest openness of heart and frankness of words. You have awaited me anxiously. They have told and written many things about me that far surpass my merits. Now I humbly present myself."[1]

He went on to describe his humble origins and how providence had moved him from his native village to travel the roads of the world, East and West. He told the congregation of diplomats, government officials, bishops, priests and laity that in beholding their patriarch they should "seek the priest, the minister of grace and nothing else, because he wishes only to express in his ministry the vocation given him by his God."[2] As he was interrupted by repeated outbursts of applause, he gently chided them, recalling that the saintly Pope Pius X, to whom he dedicated his ministry in Venice, didn't like applause either.

When the festivities were over and the thousands of well-wishers drifted back to their homes, the new patriarch turned to the editor of the diocesan newspaper and said, "Well, the bride is married off and the guests at the party have all gone away. Here I am with a big beautiful palace and do not know how to find my way around in it. Will you lead the way for me please?"[3]

Roncalli's biographers report that his years as patriarch were the happiest of his priesthood. While he was known worldwide as a great diplomat, now he would be what he wanted to be, a pastor. As a seventy-one-year-old cardinal he seemed made for the city of Venice. He felt it would be a dignified and relatively peaceful assignment, during which he would write the final chapter of his long and distinguished career. We all know that this was not going to be the end of his influence on the Catholic world.

Roncalli followed his usual protocol when he arrived in the new city. He visited Mayor Armando Gavagnin at Venice's city hall as a thank-you for the courtesy shown him on the day of his installation as patriarch. Several Council members and city officials, some of whom were socialists and communists, greeted the patriarch. He gave all of them his blessing, adding, "In this house I am at ease, even if it happens that there may be several non-Christians, but you are all considered Christians for the good work you do."[4]

His transfer to Venice didn't dilute Roncalli's pursuit of Christian Unity. Almost immediately he undertook delivering a series of lectures on the unity of the Church. After the second lecture, one of his sisters died. The editor of the local Catholic paper, who had become his confidant, suggested that he cancel the rest of the talks. He refused and requested that no public notice be made of the death. He completed the series and, at the end of the final lecture, simply asked prayers for the repose of his sister.

It happened that the wife of Eugenio Bacchion, president of the Men's Catholic Action in Venice also died that same year. Bacchion was drawn to the cardinal by mutual sorrow. The cardinal called Bacchion and said, "Tomorrow is Christmas. It will be your first Christmas with an empty place in your home. . . . Would you come tomorrow with your children and have dinner with me?"[5]

During his five years in Venice, Cardinal Roncalli was kept busy participating in feasts and festivals. His daily schedule included meeting citizens of all faiths, who visited this historic and charming city. All of his social activity, however, took second place to his ministry of souls. He jealously guarded the common touch of his priesthood. He enjoyed visiting parishes and having meals with both the local priests and the parish staff. He would remind them that he was coming "always as a Father and not as a policeman."[6] He never severed ties with his past life and experience. He maintained contact and interest in the affairs of France, Turkey and Greece. He spent the month of August each year vacationing in his home town of Sotto il Monte. He loved processing with all of the villagers on August 15, the feast of the Assumption of the Blessed Virgin Mary.

The expected and sad news of Pope Pius XII's death reached the patriarch on October 9, 1958. Knowing he would have to participate in the conclave to elect the new pope, he organized a Requiem Mass for the deceased pontiff and, with his usual calm, packed his own bag and put in it only those things that he would need for the short trip. Among the items was his cardinal's red cap (*Capa Magna)*, which he would need for the solemn requiem for the deceased pope at St. Peter's Basilica. His secretary, Monsignor Loris Capovilla, purchased two return tickets to Rome. One thing his loyal secretary noted as different about this trip was that this time the cardinal took no personal papers or books, as he had previously done even for short trips.

The last Venetian to wish the cardinal a bon voyage was the stationmaster Vittorio De Rosa. The cardinal told De Rosa he had a personal message for him, but it would have to wait until he returned from Rome. The stationmaster shocked the old man, saying, "It is my good wish that you won't be coming back."

Hesitating for a moment, Roncalli replied, "My hope is to return to Venice within fifteen days."[7]

Pius XII was the first pope to die at the papal summer residence of Castelgondolfo. His body was carried in a public procession to St. Peter's Basilica. The official nine days of public mourning began on October 11 as the cardinals from all over the world were making their way to Rome for the solemn funeral and to join the conclave to elect a successor.

October 25 was designated as the first day of the conclave. Forty-five of the fifty-four living cardinals came to Rome as the guessing game began. Who would be the next pope? As was their custom, the Roman press listed the progressive and conservative possibilities, called *papabili*. Since there was no favorite candidate, as had been the case on previous such occasions, speculation arose about choosing a transition pope of advanced age, probably a conservative who would fill the post for a short period between two longer and more active reigns.

Cardinal Roncalli fell into this category at age seventy-seven. The Catholic paper *Il Messaggero* wrote: "Roncalli is the most probable because he has never shown any definite leaning to any one group, either conservative or liberal. He is acquainted with the problems of international affairs and at seventy-seven is the right age."[8]

The forty-five cardinals received their final instructions from the secretary of *Papal Briefs to Princes,* Monsignor Bacci, to "choose a master, pastor and father. Give the Holy Roman and Universal Church a capable and suitable shepherd in the briefest possible time [some conclaves lasted several months] and with the greatest zeal, forsaking any earthly consideration and keeping your eyes on God."

Vested in their scarlet robes, the cardinals assembled in the Pauline Chapel and processed through the ancient Vatican halls into the conclave area in the Sistine Chapel. The deliberating and balloting began, with all of the cardinals bound to secrecy. All telephones to and from the conclave were silenced. The only line of communication between the cardinals and the outside world was a simple smokestack, which would be used to send up either dark or white smoke. The dark smoke would indicate that the cardinals had not yet elected a pope on the ballots held to that point. The white smoke would announce that they had chosen a pope, a Vicar of Christ. The solemn prayerful quiet of the Sistine Chapel was in stark contrast to the thousands of noisy people waiting anxiously outside in St. Peter's Square for the white smoke proclaiming "we have a new pope."

Historians do not record what really happened in this special conclave. We can only guess that Angelo Roncalli was elected not because he would be only a stop-gap interim pope, but because of his reputation as a humble servant of the Church with extraordinary diplomatic skills. The dean of the Sacred College of Cardinals probably approached and stood before Roncalli to ask, "Do you accept your election as Supreme Pontiff?"[9]

Reportedly, the seventy-seven-year-old patriarch was lost in sober thought for a moment and then responded, "I tremble and am afraid. My poorness and littleness fill me with confusion. But I see in the votes of my eminent brother cardinals the sign of God's will. Therefore I accept the election. I bow my head and bend my back to the yoke of the cross."

Cardinal Roncalli was now pope. As reported in Chapter I, he chose the name John when asked by Cardinal Tisserant, "By what name shall you be called?" He explained why he chose that name. His scarlet skullcap, signifying he was a cardinal, was removed and he received the white skullcap of the papacy. To the surprise of most of the cardinals, he placed his scarlet skullcap on the head of Monsignor di Jorio, publicly signifying that he would raise the monsignor to the rank of cardinal.[10]

The new pope retired to the sacristy, where he was vested in the papal robes. He then took his position on the throne to receive the first act of obedience and submission from the cardinals. Each cardinal mounted the steps, then knelt and kissed the pope's slipper, his knee and his hands.[11]

Felicitations from Church and civic leaders worldwide came immediately to congratulate Pope John XXIII. One of the first came from the United States President Dwight D. Eisenhower, followed by Queen Elizabeth of England, chief Rabbi of Israel Dr. Isaac Herzog, and Patriarch Alexius, the head of the Russian Orthodox Church.

The new Holy Father and his secretary Monsignor Capovilla never did use their return tickets to Venice. The worldwide press, who predicted that Pope John XXIII was going to be an interim stop-gap pope because of his age, were in for a big surprise. In just a few months after his coronation as pope, he created twenty-three new cardinals and then announced a diocesan synod and a new ecumenical council.

CHAPTER XXII

What's up with Conservatives?

In 2009 Father Michael Gilgannon, a widely respected missionary priest from the Archdiocese of Kansas City, Missouri, wrote an open letter challenging the leadership style of his spiritual leader Bishop Robert Finn. After thirty-six years of service in La Paz, Bolivia, Gilgannon was back with his family in Kansas as he recovered from cardiac surgery. During his convalescence, his colleagues in the priesthood and lay friends, most of them with Vatican II mindsets, spent many hours visiting this warm and outgoing missionary.

Gilgannon had plenty of time to catch up on all that was happening in his native United States and with the growing division in the Catholic Church, as he read local newspapers and watched television programs. He frequently tried to speak directly to Bishop Finn, but was always told by the chancery staff that the bishop was unavailable to meet him. Being a kind and sensitive individual, he did not accuse Finn of trying to avoid him. Instead, in his open letter to the bishop, he took the blame, saying, "I was very low in energy following my operation." On the other hand, he was not shy about engaging his superior in what he called "a frank and sincere dialogue," noting that only in this way will "real changes bring us to a new unity."

His letter read: "I speak of my concerns to you, Bishop, in that spirit. You have made many changes in the diocese since you came with a particular agenda. You appear to me and many priests of my generation, who lived the spirit-filled days of Vatican II, as one whose task is to reverse the changes of that great event. You have given the impression that your changes were made for the sake of a narrow 'orthodoxy,' which seems to imply that the bishops, priests and laity before you were not orthodox."[1]

This Vatican II priest was clearly upset about what had been happening throughout the Catholic world during the eighties and nineties. Bishop Finn was not an aberration. He typified those bishops chosen by the *Congregation for Bishops* who were more comfortable in the top-down authoritative system of the pre-Vatican II era.

In the letter Gilgannon explained his upset over the way Bishop Finn had totally changed the Diocesan Lay Formation Center by terminating its quite competent teaching team. Gilgannon remembered the center's original form as a model for all Catholic dioceses in the United States. He criticized the bishop for naming the most conservative college in the country, Ave Maria University, and its theological school in Florida as the only source of lay formation in the diocese. He advised his boss that there were several other national resources available on a theological continuum, from conservative to liberal, all within Catholic orthodoxy.[2]

Conservative Bishops and laity like Finn differ with progressive Catholics such as Gilgannon on social issues. They are in general opposed to any national health plan that provides health care insurance to all U.S. citizens. Progressive Catholics ask, "Can America claim to be the most powerful nation and number one in the world if forty-seven million of its citizens, those in low-income families and families living below the poverty level, have no health insurance?"

Similarly, for most of this century conservative Catholics have had a battle with progressives on how to resolve the polarity of beliefs and practices within Catholicism. Chicago's Cardinal Joseph L. Bernardin, a church leader highly respected by progressives, made a valiant effort before his untimely death at age sixty-eight on November 14, 1996. In consultation with a variety of U.S. Church leaders associated with the National Pastoral Life Center, Bernardin published a statement intended to help restore Church unity and vitality.

The article, published on August 12, 1996, was entitled "Called to be Catholic: Church in a Time of Peril." Bernardin wrote, "For three decades the church has been divided by different responses to the Second Vatican Council and to the tumultuous years that followed it. . . . But, even as conditions changed, party lines have hardened. A mood of suspicion and acrimony hangs over those most active in the church's life; at moments it seems to have infiltrated the ranks of bishops." The statement called for open and honest discussion on issues such as the changing roles of women, the meaning of human sexuality, and the gap between church teachings and the convictions of many faithful in several areas of morality.[3]

The ink was barely dry on Cardinal Bernardin's printed statement when then-Cardinal Law of Boston replied on the same day. He described Bernardin's statement as flawed and "not very helpful." In Law's view, Bernardin's article called for an impossible dialogue—between *Magisterium* teaching and the beliefs of the Pastoral Life Centers that were "dissent from the authoritative teaching of the Church [that could] not be dialogued away." Law argued, "Dissent either yields to assent or the conflict remains irresolvable." It seems that Cardinal Law ignored the lessons of the *Documents of Vatican Council II* just as he later ignored his civil and moral duties to report criminal pedophile priests to civil authorities.[4]

The Vatican II priests and laity now condemn the conservative bishops for proposing a one-issue public dialogue on political candidates and platforms that denies the Catholic tradition of social teaching on a wide range of issues. Furthermore, they want the bishops to advocate respect for all human life, called the "Seamless Garment" by Chicago Cardinal Joseph Bernardin in his widely published presentation *Consistent Ethic of Life* at St. Louis University on March 11, 1984.

To Gilgannon and his followers, the position of conservative bishops represents only a small segment of the Church membership at the expense of validly influencing a wider segment of the American public. They resent being lumped together with those opposed to the defense of life just because they favor the broad social teachings of the Catholic Church.

The progressive group of clergy and laity also now challenge those conservative bishops for failing to be pro-life on the issue of the Iraq and Afghanistan wars. They furthermore ask the bishops why they don't object to the post-conscription practice of hiring the poor and the marginalized to fight and die in these "unwise and unjust wars." The progressives point out that all Americans, both rich and poor, were drafted for the Vietnam War, while today's system simply hires the disenfranchised to fight and die to protect our freedom. Father Gilgannon ends his letter, saying, "Our church is more divided among leadership and faithful than at any other time in my life of seventy-six years and my fifty-one years as a priest."

The conservative movement in the Catholic Church didn't begin in the seventies and eighties as a reaction to the liberalism promulgated in the Vatican II documents. As noted previously, long before Vatican Council II, the Reverend Father Marcial Maciel Degollado founded the very conservative Legion of Christ. Vatican officials were well aware of its conservative theology and secretive rules and allowed themselves to be blinded by the mushrooming growth, as it boasted of hundreds of men ordained to the priesthood and thousands of seminarians studying in colleges and seminaries in Mexico, Italy, Spain and the United States. The most disappointing part of the story is that the charismatic founder became a hero to the Vatican *Curia*, probably because, like their own operation, his *modus operandi* lacked transparency and demanded secrecy and blind loyalty to him the founder.

One wonders now whether there is a correlation between the fall of the Legion and the Church's present embarrassment related to its priest-pedophile disaster. Several months ago, one cardinal confidentially shared his view with me that what is needed is a total purification of the Church from top to bottom. If and when that happens, we will all know that the Holy Spirit is once again guiding the Church. I ask, "What would Pope John XXIII say and do now to establish transparency in all segments of Church law if he were still the Vicar of Christ? What steps do all of us, both religious (priests, brothers, sisters) and lay, need to take to re-establish loyalties to Jesus rather than loyalties to Church leaders who put protection of their own power over the safety of children?"

CHAPTER XXIII

Blessed John Paul II: Awe and Ambivalence

As reported in Chapter XVII, in 1986 I had the privilege of concelebrating Mass with the Holy Father John Paul II along with several other Irish-born priests. I was moved by John Paul's meditative preparation for the memorial celebration of Jesus' final supper with his disciples. I don't believe it was a blind leap of faith for me to realize I was about to celebrate the Eucharist with a living saint. He gave 100 percent attention as one of our fellow priests read the Scriptures of the day's liturgy. Several of us noticed that he actually shuddered at Peter's denial, saying, "I will never leave you, even though all the others do. . . . I will never say that [I do not know you] even if I have to die with you" (Mt. 26:33-35). John Paul was acting as if he himself feared betraying Jesus, his Master.

His life and ministry to the world, both Catholic and non-Catholic, as Jesus Christ's Vicar on earth, created such an outpouring of admiration, respect and devotion that his successor Pope Benedict XVI felt obligated to waive the mandatory five years of waiting before his beatification. The projected attendance at the beatification ceremony in St. Peter's Square was one million. As a testimony to his overwhelming popularity and his history of always generating large and enthusiastic crowds, the actual attendance exceeded the projected attendance by half a million people.

"He was like a king to us, like a father," said a twenty-eight-year-old woman named Marynka from Poland. Weeping, she added, "I hope these emotions remain with us for a very long time."[1]

Pope Benedict, speaking at the beatification, said, "John Paul has shown the strength of a titan. This exemplary son of Poland helped believers throughout the world not to be afraid to be called Christians, to belong to the Church, to speak of the Gospel." Others would call John Paul a titan for standing up to Nazism and Communism in his native Poland.[2]

Journalist John L. Allen, Jr., reminds us that while the Catholic world was in awe of John Paul II, there is some ambivalence about his canonization as a saint. On the one hand, he remains a popular and revered figure, capable of generating vast and enthusiastic crowds as well as global media interest. On the other, he is still a sign of contradiction in some quarters, stirring criticism for various aspects of his almost twenty-seven years of papacy, including the clergy sexual abuse crisis. At the same time, progressives "charge that John Paul's papacy reversed the spirit of reform associated with the Second Vatican Council."[3] Fellow Irishman Thomas Groome, professor of theology and religious education at Boston College, said, "There are responsible people . . . who would say he launched a reform of reforms and led us backward rather than forward. Many Catholics feel he did not embrace the spirit of renewal and reform heralded by the Second Vatican Council." Groome charged that "John Paul was a better pope for the world than for the Church."[4]

While Cardinal Francis George of Chicago recalled John Paul's 104 visits abroad as the evangelizer of the world, he said, "He took it upon himself to preach the Gospel of Christ to the world."[5] Many progressive Catholics would be more forgiving of John Paul's inadequacies as world church leader if he had not appointed so many conservative bishops worldwide. Others have difficulty understanding and accepting how such an intelligent pope and his close associate, the now-Cardinal Stanislaw Dziwisz of Krakow, Poland, were outwitted by the voracious sociopath Father Marcial Maciel Degollado of the Legion of Christ. As reported earlier, the cardinal refused to cooperate when journalists sought to tell the story.

Joshua J. McElwee, a journalist with the *National Catholic Reporter*, conducted a series of interviews with prominent Catholics after the January 14, 2011, announcement that Pope John Paul II was going to be beatified. He discovered a tension between those who desired to recognize the late pope's holiness and critics of his actions during his papacy. While nobody challenged the news of the official declaration of the miraculous healing of forty-nine-year-old Sister Marie Simon-Pierre attributed to John Paul, others were not comfortable with the speed of his beatification. Father Richard Vega, president of the National Federation of Priests' Councils, said that the normal five-year period would have allowed more time to examine John Paul's relationship with Maciel, "such as whether John Paul's dealings with Maciel clouded his vision."[6]

Benedictine Sister Joan Chittister commented that John Paul's "attitude toward clerical sexual abuse of children embodied the worst kind of clericalism. The least the Church could do in respect to those who have already suffered insult at the hands of the Church is to let the perspective of time decide whether or not canonization is in order."[7]

Anthony Padovano, who holds a doctorate in sacred theology from the Pontifical Gregorian University and is now professor at Ramapo College (NJ), said the late pontiff's use of power during his papacy set a bad example for "the kind of life you expect the people in the Church to emulate." He added, "The witness of John Paul II should not be presented as a model for what a Christian is supposed to do."[8] On the positive side, Benedictine Father Anscar Chupungco from the Philippines Episcopal Commission on Liturgy praised John Paul's visits to developing countries and his emphasis on integrating local customs and cultural traditions into the Liturgy. Chupungco said, "I dare call him the 'father of liturgical enculturation.' I would like to regard his beatification as an affirmation of his liturgical ministry to the local churches outside the Western Hemisphere."[9]

The bottom line is that, for several months prior to the beatification, Vatican officials insisted that "the saint-making process isn't a judgment on how John Paul administered the Church, but rather whether he lived a life of Christian virtue.[10] John Paul's former spokesperson, Joaquin Navarro-Valls, did not hesitate to brush aside the naysayers who accused Pope Benedict XVI of rushing the beatification. He also dismissed the assertion by the Survivors Network of those Abused by Priests (SNAP) that "in more than twenty-five years, as the most powerful figure on the planet, John Paul did almost nothing to safeguard the kids across the world."[11]

Navarro-Valls was adamant, saying, "This is not a historical judgment [on Pope John Paul II's papacy]. That might take centuries. But to be aware, to know well the Christian virtues in his life, which is what beatification is all about, that's clear." Then he asked rhetorically, "Once the virtues are clear, why wait?"[12]

I spent many years in the priesthood advocating Family Life Education, Pre-Marriage programs and ways in which the Catholic Church could facilitate the family as the agent of change in society, rather than as the "victim" of every whim created by a needy society. For those reasons I find myself a fan of Blessed John Paul. From the beginning of his priesthood, the "Family" played a central role in the future pope's pastoral ministry.

Ludmila and Stanislaw Grygiel, two young followers who knew him as Cardinal Karol Wojtyla while he served the people of Krakow, wrote the article *Love is Possible* for the magazine *Columbia*. They recall how the future pope missed his family. His mom died when he was only nine. His older soul brother, Edmund, died of scarlet fever. Edmund was a physician and role model for the young Karol. His passing was very traumatic. "Karol was then raised by his father, who was both caring and demanding." To add to the loss of his mom and his only sibling, his dad died in 1941 when Karol was just twenty-one years old.[13]

According to Ludmila and Stanislaw, the future pope spent a lot of time visiting and ministering to young families following his ordination to the priesthood in 1946, "sharing their joys and sorrows which we frequently experience ourselves."[14] Father Wojtyla was apparently a good listener and learned from these young couples about their struggles living in Poland under a communist regime.

Since Blessed John Paul II's death in 2005, people ask, "What is this Holy Father's legacy?" Cardinal Carlo Caffarra, now the archbishop of Bologna, Italy, gives us the answer: "The Holy Father was profoundly convinced that the defense and promotion of marriage and family life was one of the most important elements of the mission of the Church in the third millennium." John Paul chose Caffarra as president of the Pontifical John Paul Institute for Studies on Marriage and Family, which he founded in 1988. The concept of such an institute was the result of the 1980 Synod of Bishops on the Family, as well as the desire of John Paul II, "who entrusted the institute's work to Mary under the title Our Lady of Fatima."[15]

Prior to the establishment of the institute at the Lateran University in Rome, John Paul was in the process of presenting his catechesis on the theology of the body, which became part of the curriculum of the institute and which expanded to several continents in the following years. Cardinal Caffarra explained the depth of John Paul's commitment to the cause of Marriage and Family Life, which has now become his legacy. Caffarra explained, "He also said that this defense and promotion must occur at the most profound level of thought and reflection—scientific, philosophical and theological."[16] Since the establishment of the institute in 1988, it has expanded to include seven sessions and now has four associated centers.

While many of those interviewed were critical of the "speed of John Paul's beatification," very few disputed his personal piety. "They took opposition, rather, to the image and thrust of his papacy and the priority of his sainthood." Father Charles Curran, professor of theology at Southern Methodist University in Dallas, said that although he had no objection to the news of the beatification, the Church "would be a lot better off if we stopped canonizing popes, bishops, clergy and religious." Other interviewees, such as Mercy Sister Theresa Kane, said that other causes like that of Archbishop Oscar Romero should have taken precedence and that the beatification of the late pope was "somewhat premature." Padovano said, "Personal piety is less important than the kind of public sense of the individual the Church has. . . . Canonization is a public action that is not just dealing with personal piety, but is looking at the kind of behavior that it sees should be emulated."[17]

Blessed John Paul's legacy contains horrendous negatives, like failing to protect innocent children from pedophile priests and to discipline bishops who transferred these predators from parish to parish.

His being outwitted by Father Marcial Marcel will remain a mystery for many years to come.

John Paul's biographer George Weigel summarized the positives of his legacy when he wrote, "He made Christianity interesting and compelling at a moment when many in the western world imagined that they had 'outgrown' the 'need' for religious faith. . . . He gave new energy to Catholicism in America at a time of lethargy; and he inspired many American evangelicals with his unapologetic preaching of the Gospel."[18] Millions of Catholics worldwide will cherish images of Blessed John Paul's celebration of masses in stadiums and parks for thousands of the faithful, role in the fall of the Berlin wall, and unapologetic defense of traditional Church teaching on marriage, family, sexual morality and the Virgin Mary as Mother of the Church.

CHAPTER XXIV
The Challenge Facing Neo-Catholics

Before we pull the trigger and launch Vatican Council III, it is only fair that we share with our readers the probable obstacles progressive Catholics will encounter. Or is our Catholic Church in such a crisis now that cardinals, bishops, *periti,* elected priests, elected laymen and women (both religious and lay), representing the four corners of the world, should be invited immediately to Rome by the incarnated spirit of Pope John XXIII?

To gain authentic insights into how conservative Catholics view the Church and how they would describe today's crisis in their Church, I turned to the expertise of a reputable conservative theologian, Dr. Alan Schreck, chairman of the theology department at the Franciscan University of Steubenville. Dr. Schreck not only speaks for the Church *Magisterium,* but he also has the mandatum from his local bishop that allows him to teach theology at the university. Among the several books he has authored, I studied *Vatican II: The Crisis and the Promise,* which the outspoken conservative Archbishop of Philadelphia Charles J. Chaput describes as a "lucid, insightful and a wonderfully absorbing guide to understanding the key themes of the Second Vatican Council."[1]

I am impressed with Schreck's honest attempt at authenticity in analyzing both progressive and conservative Catholicism. I am, however, also mindful that in order for Schreck to retain his professorship at a Catholic college he is forbidden to criticize the *Magisterium,* which I am free to do. Dr. Schreck tells us how some Catholics "reject outright the authority of the Council or particular points of its teaching and tradition. Some see themselves as the 'loyal opposition,' still deeply committed to the Catholic Church, but genuinely convinced that some of the teaching or direction of the Council was erroneous or misguided."[2]

The English writer Michael Davies, writing in the mid-1970s, blamed the Council for all of the problems of the Church. He had the audacity to write that "no rational person can deny that up until the present Vatican II has produced no good fruits."[3]

In their 2002 book *The Great Façade: Vatican II and the Regime of Novelty in the Roman Catholic Church*, the authors Christopher A. Ferrara and Thomas E. Woods launched what Schreck called a frontal assault on Vatican Council II. The authors claimed that Neo-Catholics believe "that with the advent of the Second Vatican Council a new sort of orthodoxy arose in the Church: an orthodoxy stripped of any link to ecclesiastical traditions, once considered an untouchable sacred trust. . . . Whether he knows it or not the Neo-Catholic has broken with tradition."[4]

These two authors don't even try to mask their disdain for the Catholic Charismatic Renewal program and, according to Schreck, make "no pretence of presenting them with justice and charity."[5] These two authors, who profess to be traditional Catholics, totally disregard the many statements of Popes Paul VI and John Paul II that encourage and recommend the Catholic Charismatic Renewal, which finds its doctrinal basis in Scripture and Catholic tradition as well as in the teachings of Vatican II.[6]

Davies, author of several conservative anti-Council books, including *The Second Vatican Council and Religious Liberty,* believed that Vatican Council II was a pastoral council whose teachings were not infallible and hence not demanding assent from faithful Catholics. The difficulty with such critics of Vatican II is that they overlook Paul VI's directive that these documents, even if they express only the authority of the *Magisterium*, "must be accepted with docility." If you were to follow the traditional critics of Vatican Council II, you would believe only in documents that were defined as infallible.[7]

Dr. Schreck tells us that the dissenters he has described "would be angered by the suggestion that they are disloyal Catholics or that they are a 'problem' in the Church."[8] They claim they are simply responding to the real crisis in the Church, which they identify as a loss of true Catholic identity and a betrayal of authentic Catholic teaching. It is clear that dissenters like Michael Davies will always be against any reform in the Church and will cause a lot of conflict with the Neo-Catholics, who are firm believers in the spirit of Vatican Council II, particularly as enunciated in the *Pastoral Constitution on the Church in the Modern World, Gaudium et Spes.* While some progressive Catholics have reservations about Blessed John Paul II's fast track to canonization, all Neo-Catholics support him in his staunch support of Vatican Council II and in his declaration of religious liberty as enunciated in the Council's *Declaration of Religious Liberty, Dignitatis Humanae.* Literally, all people were given the right to proclaim their particular religion and practice it as long as the religion didn't violate the basic human rights.[9] Opponents of Vatican II believe that only the true religion (Catholicism) has an unrestricted right to religious freedom.

Neo-Catholics see the present crisis of pedophile priests and the cover-up by the hierarchy as the failure of the hierarchy and the Vatican to admit to the world that they erred in handling the crisis. The hierarchy's lack of transparency and blame of the press for exaggerating the sins of a small percentage in the priesthood has caused much anger and confusion among moderate and progressive Catholics, who realize the bishops were actually covering up crimes in the priesthood. Meanwhile the critics of Vatican II ignore the criminality. They blame several factors: the widespread confusion over the meaning and nature of the priesthood, disagreement about mandatory celibacy for priests, and a dramatic drop in vocations. All of these factors are due, according to author James Hitchcock, to John Paul II's failure to distinguish between hope and optimism following Vatican Council II.[10]

Progressives believe that Vatican II's call for renewal of religious life was necessary. In progressives' view, any resulting divisions in religious communities were caused by some community members' resistance to the *aggiornamento* and wish to remain in the authoritative, conservative culture of the forties and fifties. Progressives became excited about liturgical renewal, including having the Mass celebrated in their native languages versus Latin, which they didn't understand. They were enthused about women becoming more involved in the Mass as readers, Eucharistic ministers, or altar servers.

As Schreck reports, conservatives claim that the liturgical changes caused "mass confusion."[11] (Pun intended) According to them, the new language of the Liturgy, the liturgical music, the new art, architecture, and so forth, turned people off, causing an unprecedented drop in weekend Mass attendance, "while Sunday became just another day of work and worldly activity."[12] Progressives blame the drop in Mass attendance, by women in particular, as directly related to the realization that denying the priesthood to women is based more on chauvinism in the hierarchy than on any evidence from Sacred Scripture.

Progressive Catholics believe that children should be educated about God's gift of human sexuality, first in the home and later in Catholic schools. Conservatives argue that sex education encourages sexual intimacy among teenagers. They go so far as to take their children out of Family Life classes in the school and will cooperate only if the major emphasis in the course is on total sexual abstinence until after marriage.

Progressive Catholics follow the Vatican II recommendation to dialogue with non-Catholic Christians and members of Orthodox congregations as an important step toward Christian Unity. Conservatives, according to Dr. Schreck, see "dialogue with these groups to be simply building relationships with them," further claiming that "these discussions deny and distort or compromise Catholic doctrines."[13] To put it simply, conservative Catholics believe that there is only one true religion (i.e., Catholicism) and that people of all different faiths should convert to it. The schema on religious liberty, *Dignitatis Humanae*, in the *Documents of Vatican II* disagrees.

Conservative Catholics do not dissent from the teachings of the Church's *Magisterium*, because it "leaves the faithful confused about Catholic beliefs and about who to believe and who to follow." Progressives believe that renewal and reform in the Church is necessary at different periods of history to deal with crises such as those we have currently.

At this time, the Association of Catholic Priests in Ireland and the People of God are joined together in prayer and dialogue to advise the bishops in Ireland regarding reforms needed to purify the Catholic faith. Their main target is the scandal of the bishops who choose to protect the good name of the Church rather than the safety of the children sexually abused by pedophile priests. These reform groups know that change is going to come from the bottom up, with the Holy Spirit guiding the reform, just as he promised to guide the Church (Galatians 5:16-18).

Pope Benedict XVI expressed the belief that we have to be honest, "we must speak . . . of a crisis of faith and of the Church. We can overcome it only if we face up to it forthrightly."[14] Pope John XXIII warned us, as he addressed the participants of Vatican II at the opening ceremony in 1962, that recognizing the Church as in crisis was not to be interpreted as being a prophet of doom, but rather as being a realist. Schreck adds a little humor: "We cannot afford to be like the emperor who prided himself on his beautiful new clothes when he actually had none on."

According to moderate conservatives, the trouble with Catholicism is not from the teachings of Vatican Council II but from the distortions, partial presentations and misunderstandings of the Council's teaching. They then go on to accuse the Neo-Catholics of doing things in the "name" of Vatican II, or according to the "spirit" of Vatican II. Moderate conservatives claim that this "spirit" is nowhere to be found (or accurately found) in the Council documents. The "spirit" of Vatican Council II is usually interpreted by progressives as openness to the world and to new ideas and approaches, such as democratization of the Church.

Pope John Paul II called an extraordinary Synod of Bishops in 1985 to assess the effects and implementation of Vatican II twenty years after the Council closed. When the bishops listed several problems that affected the Church at large, they suggested a four-stage follow up:

1. Organize a complete study of the Vatican II documents.
2. Learn how to assimilate the Council into our lives.
3. Realize how affirming the documents can be.
4. Create a plan on how to implement the documents.[15]

There is no way to know how familiar Pope John Paul II was with the next crisis to hit the Catholic Church after the Council ended. Did the heads of the Congregations and the *Curia* shield him from the pedophile crisis, or, worse still, did he know that many of his own subject bishops chose to protect the good name of the Church and simply transfer the criminal priests to another assignment? We do know that, for whatever reason, thousands of innocent children's lives were forever damaged.

The Neo-Catholics point to a powerful statement in the documents themselves that seem prophetic. In the *Pastoral Constitution on the Church in the Modern World, Gaudium et Spes* we read: "By the power of the Holy Spirit the Church is the faithful spouse of the Lord and will never fail to be a sign of salvation in the world; but it is by no means unaware that down through the centuries there have been among its members, both clerical and lay, some who have been disloyal to the Spirit of God. Today as well, the Church is not blind to the discrepancy between the message it proclaims and the human weakness of those to whom the Gospel has been entrusted. Whatever the historic judgment on those shortcomings, we cannot ignore them and we must combat them earnestly, lest they hinder the spread of the Gospel" (*GS* IV: 76).

Echoing *Gaudium et Spes*, the Neo-Catholics of the world call on the Vatican, the *Curia*, and the heads of the Congregations and bishops of the world to live up to the "actual words" (not just the spirit) of the Vatican Council II documents and "combat them" (the crimes of pedophile priests and the cover-up) "earnestly, lest they hinder the spread of the Gospel."

CHAPTER XXV

Repairing our Broken Church

What would Uncle Father Michael say if he read the editorial in the *Irish Voice* on August 24, 2011? The headline read "ARREST BISHOP FOR COVER-UP." The text continued: "The spectacle of Bishop John Magee [the former secretary to three popes] abjectly apologizing this week for his utter failure to curb pedophile priests in his Cork diocese [Cloyne] makes the blood run cold. Magee bolted out of the country when the Cloyne report was made public. It was a devastating document, detailing in great precision the horrific cover-up. Magee has admitted his actions. . . . Magee is culpable for placing children in harm's way, and he has now admitted this. The next step should be to arrest the bishop."[1]

Bishop Magee returned to Ireland to his parish house in County Cork. He later issued a statement that he was "very willing" to meet privately with the victims and apologize to the priests of Cloyne. He admitted, "I let the many good priests of the diocese down," and later, on Radio Television Eireann (RTE), he said, "To the victims, I say I am truly horrified by the abuse that they suffered. . . . On bended knee I beg forgiveness. I am sorry."[2]

Father Michael would say that, if the bishop had knowingly broken the civil law, then the civil authority should hold him responsible. My personal concern is for the victims of sexual abuse and for the faithful priests in the Diocese of Cloyne, including my classmate Father Dan Gould. I have empathy for the faithful Irish bishops like Diarmuid Martin of the Archdiocese of Dublin, whom the editorial describes as "those bishops and priests who do their best to act on their Holy Orders. Will they too be tarred by the refusal to cast out this evil among them?"[3]

The editorial compares the case of John Magee in Ireland with the arrest of Monsignor William Lynn in Philadelphia, "for exactly the same criminal behavior in failing to act against the pedophile priests in his archdiocese." The editorial observes that "Lynn is finding the definition of criminal behavior when it comes to abusing kids does not stop at the perpetrator, but also includes the enabler."[4]

The issue for all of us who love and belong to the Church is identifying what steps must be taken to reform the Church. The editorial focuses on reform, not just on the renewal or purification that some bishops have talked about. The editorial claims that, by making an example of Bishop Magee, the State is helping the Church regain its reputation by differentiating between faithful bishops and priests and criminals like Magee who have "scarred countless lives."[5]

Is the Catholic Church in Ireland salvageable? The task of repairing our broken Church is multifaceted. The *Congregation for the Doctrine of the Faith* began the task in 2010. Before then, the Code of Canon Law reserved to the pope all cases involving accusations of violations of the Church's criminal laws by bishops and those above them. Now, the *Congregation for the Doctrine of the Faith* has the right to judge members of the ruling class (cardinals, bishops and papal legates). This change was in response to the accusation that bishops accused of sexually abusing children were given a free pass. Father Thomas Doyle, a Canon lawyer and addiction therapist, criticizes the Congregation for leaving a serious gap in the new Canon because it excludes the bishops' responsibility to report the criminal acts of clerics to civil authority. In his judgment and mine, "the cover-up and dishonesty of not reporting crimes of sexual abuse is a crime in itself. The cover-up by the bishops and cardinals had a more devastating effect on the reputation of the Church than the sexual crimes themselves."[6]

In order to repair our broken Church we also need to question secrecy. Vatican spokesman Father Federico Lombardi says, "We have to maintain secrecy to safeguard the dignity of all the people involved." To which Doyle replies, "This is a lame excuse for the Vatican's obsession with image. Historically, totalitarian regimes dispense their peculiar version of justice behind closed doors. If Lombardi's rationale [of a closed door policy] reflects the official policy, then it seems everybody's dignity is respected except the victims." Doyle notes that Lombardi's explanation is remarkable for one reason only: "He [Lombardi] admits that the public outcry, which includes the secular media coverage, had an impact on the pope and other Vatican officials."[7]

Prior to 2001, the Vatican and most conservative Catholics in the United States and Ireland accused the media critics of being anti-Catholic or dismissed their criticism as irrelevant. Following the disastrous report on the mishandling of the crisis in the Cloyne diocese in July 2011, the government of Ireland initiated a mini-war, without parallel in Irish history, with the Vatican. The substance of the mini-war is not relevant here except to report on statements made by Taoiseach (Prime Minister) Enda Kenny. Speaking before the Irish Parliament on July 22, 2011, Kenny said the government authorized the study called the Cloyne Report, which "exposes an attempt by the Holy See to frustrate an inquiry in a sovereign democratic republic as late as three years ago." Continuing his disparagement, Kenny said, "The report excavates the dysfunction, disconnections, elitism and the narcissism that dominate the Vatican to this day."[8]

More startling was the near-universal praise Kenny received even from members of the Irish hierarchy. Archbishop Martin of Dublin said he was "impressed by the emotion" of Kenny's speech. Martin spoke of "a 'cabal' in the Vatican who were trying to undermine and are refusing to understand what was being done in terms of child protection."[9]

The Vatican's initial response was to recall papal nuncio Archbishop Giuseppe Leanza to the Vatican for "consultations" to help prepare the Vatican's response to the Kenny accusations. Irish diocesan priest Father Ignatius O'Donovan, when interviewed by the *Drogheda Independent* newspaper in July 2011, admitted, "I don't think it is finished yet and I speak for myself when I wonder if I am part of an inept and incompetent institution." Then he added, "People have been saying to me 'how can all this have happened,' and I know it will hit many mass numbers more. However, the damning part is that the Church did not keep its own guidelines, never mind the State's guidelines." He finished the interview with feelings similar to my own: "My feeling is sadness, most of all for those who suffered. The cover-ups were the biggest sins of all."[10]

I don't believe a renewal by purification of the Catholic Church will be sufficient to repair Father Michael's broken Church. It will take a reformation, going back to the Scripture and reorganizing the servant Church established by Jesus. It will take reestablishing the church as the People of God, as enunciated by Pope John XXIII before his death in June 1963. Father Tom Doyle writes that "the main problem with the Vatican's latest attempt at damage control is that they continue to deny the fundamental issue: the nature of the clericalized, monarchical structure of the institutional Church and its systematic dismantling of the reality of church as the People of God."[11]

Likewise, in an article on July 24, 2011, he wrote: "The clerical culture that cannot comprehend the depth of the evil and destruction it has enabled has failed to internalize the reality that in this twenty-first century sacrificing the welfare of innocent children to maintain an image and power of an ecclesiastical aristocracy is a disgrace that will be a catalyst for an inevitable and profound change in the nature of the institutional Church." Continuing to critique the relationship between the Catholic Church in Ireland and Irish society, the author says, "The rapid disintegration of the absolute control of the Irish hierarchy over Irish society is the result not of the lack of faith of the Irish people, as some ecclesiastical leadership would have us believe, but in the lack of fidelity of the leadership to the people they have sworn to serve."[12]

To renew the Irish Church's loyalty to Benedict XVI does not mean we condemn Taoiseach Kenny's blast at the Vatican. It will mean that a dialogue between both parties must be initiated. If Pope Benedict seeks guidance from the archbishop of Dublin, he will be told to follow Bishop Magee's example of confessing publicly that he erred in not protecting the lives of innocent children.

The issue of the Vatican's secrecy and concern for the Church's reputation ahead of reporting the crimes of pedophile clergy was confronted by Martin when he challenged, "Tell the truth and it will set us all free."

What will a reformed Catholic Church look like? Will it still have the monarchical-hierarchical structure that exercises its power in secret, holding onto its past with an emphasis on image rather than service to the weak and needy of our society? Will the new Church fulfill the dream of John XXIII, who envisioned a servant Church comprised of laity, men and women serving side by side with servant priests, bishops and cardinals? Will the people of Rome see a future pope taking a walk through the streets of the eternal city as John XXIII did, earning himself the nickname of "Johnny Walker"? Will we ever again have a servant pope who regularly visits the prisons of Rome as John XXIII and John Paul II did?

"Father Michael, intercede for us as we pray and work toward a reformed church headed by a man or woman who walks in the footsteps of St. Peter the fisherman."

CHAPTER XXVI
Resolution and Reform versus Revolution

"Anyone who has come to the decision that Rome is on the wrong track must leave the Catholic Church."[1] So spoke Cardinal Christoph Schönborn of Vienna on August 10, 2010, while addressing the Austrian Priests Initiative (API), a committee of three hundred reform-minded priests. Founded in 2006 by Monsignor Helmut Schüller, a leading churchman and former vicar general under Schönborn, the group issued an "Appeal to Disobedience" in June 2011, declaring that they were taking positive action on a list of reforms such as distributing Holy Communion to everyone who approached the altar in good faith, including divorced Catholics who had remarried without an annulment. They also spoke out publicly in support of the ordination of women and married men. Twelve thousand lay Catholics professed their support of the initiative.

Bishops and theologians are disconnected. The chasm between Church teachings and pastoral practice must be addressed if the Catholic Church is to survive and continue its evangelization. A poll taken among Austrian Catholics reports that the majority do not want the debate to end with one group winning and the other losing. They want both sides to negotiate a resolution. Many interpret the cardinal's statement on August 10, 2010, to be an ultimatum: obey the Church or get out of the priesthood. Archdiocesan spokesperson Michael Prüller said, "The situation is not as dramatic as the Austrian media make it seem. The cardinal's statement is nothing like that. There has been no talk of sanctions, no ultimatum and no talk of punishment. There will be an ongoing debate and there has to be a discussion on the underlying issues."[2]

Cardinal Schönborn was ordained a priest of the Dominican Order at age twenty-five by Franz Cardinal König. Like many of the bishops we reported on earlier, Schönborn became an academic after a brief pastoral experience as student pastor at the University of Graz in 1973, before his appointment two years later to associate professor of dogma at the University of Fribourg in Switzerland.[3] He was appointed auxiliary bishop of Vienna in 1991 at the age of forty-six. Schönborn was on his way to becoming one of the youngest cardinals in the world. This potential pope taught dogmatic theology and served on international commissions that dialogued with other Christian Churches and Orthodox Christians for most of his priesthood.

His critics claim he lacks sufficient grassroots experience in serving lay Catholics at a parish level to head a conflicted worldwide community as pastor of the Catholic world. Schönborn is not giving in to the API. He plans to continue a dialogue with them even though the Conference of Religious Superiors believes the controversy cannot be resolved by Schönborn alone. They see a possible schism on the horizon and they want the dialogue to include a larger group of people.[4] The religious orders must be included, as half of the priests who serve the Catholic population in Austria belong to religious communities. Abbot Martin Felhofer of Schlagl Abbey said, "Everyone . . . bishops, abbots, religious and representatives of the API . . . must sit down together and discuss these problems."[5]

Lay Catholic groups in Austria are seeking other ways to reform the Church and bridge the gap between Church teaching and pastoral practices. They are not depending on Schonborn and the API. Franz Köberl, the director of Caritas, told the Austrian State Radio on September 3, 2011, that the Church reform debate was not confined to Austria. Caritas is aware of the Association of Catholic Priests in Ireland, which is demanding reform from the Irish Catholic hierarchy and the Vatican. Luitgard Derschmidt, the head of Austrian Catholic Action, which represents five hundred thousand lay Catholics, says she realizes that the API "has had enough" and that Catholic Action shares their concerns. Her focus is on an issue that I believe is going to be the principal matter. She says her understanding of that the API's position is "not so much a calling to disobedience, but for a higher obedience to conscience and to God."[6]

Progressive Catholics, who are the majority of registered Catholics in Austria, Ireland and the United States, want the Church to lift the ban preventing women and married men from ordination. They claim that they have the documents of Vatican Council II on their side, while 70 percent of Catholics in Austria believe that the Church leaders are an important moral authority.

The *Documents of Vatican II* are clear in discussing the role and dignity of man's conscience in making moral decisions. Paragraph 16 of the *Pastoral Constitution on the Church in the Modern World* states: *"Deep within his conscience, man discovers a law which he has not laid upon himself but which he must obey. Its voice, ever calling him to love and to do what is good and to avoid evil, tells him inwardly at the right moment: do this, shun that. . . . His conscience is man's most secret core and his sanctuary. . . . Through this loyalty to conscience, Christians are joined to other men in the search for the truth and for the right solution to so many moral problems which arise both in the life of individuals and from social relationships"* (GS 1).

Dr. Liam McDaid, the newly consecrated bishop of the Diocese of Clogher, County Monaghan, Ireland, took a very different stance than some of his episcopal colleagues when he addressed his congregation on the day of his installation as bishop on May 6, 2010. He spoke of the terrible failure involving child abuse which society has "forced the Irish Catholics to address." He said, "The surgeon's knife has been painful but necessary. A lot of evil and poison has been excised. There comes a time when the surgeon's knife has done what it can is put away and a regime of rehabilitation for the patient is put in place. We have been brought to our knees but maybe that is no bad thing." Then he went on to surprise Cardinal Brady (the primate of all Ireland), his fellow bishops, his family and the congregation when he added, "Jesus made no room in the Church for privilege, earthly pomp or power or lording over anyone. . . . So while society keeps the mirror in front of us and rightly checks that we are sincere in our intentions and efforts towards rehabilitation, can I invite you priests and people of the Diocese of Clogher to join me in a repentant return to the well of Salvation?"[7]

The good news is that Bishop McDaid kept his word and followed through on his invitation by attending the fifth gathering of the Association of Catholic Priests (ACP) of Clogher on August 31, 2011. He listened and supported the twelve diocesan priests who participated. The priests shared how with "heavy hearts" they were setting sail into another new year of parish life and ministry. Their priestly identity had been shaken, but they knew that their struggles in no way compared with the emotional pain suffered by the victims of child abuse. Expressing their appreciation for having the ACP there to support them, they realized that they were not alone in their difficulties. They talked about the crisis of faith in Ireland and the increased sense of negativity.

One priest shared that "there appears to be a little hunger for faith, much of this may be because our Church has been found wanting. Morale among the clergy is low and the new translation of the missal does very little to lift us up."[8] The only negative reported from the Clogher ACP meetings is that less than one third of the diocesan priests are participating in them.

I feel very proud that the Association of Catholic Priests from my native country is taking such a prominent role in the reformation of the Catholic Church and in the implementation of the vision and teaching of Vatican Council II. I believe they will never support a schism from the Vatican, but their collaboration with other ACP organizations in Europe and similar organizations worldwide in hope of Church reform looks more promising daily. Like the Austrian Priests Initiative, the Irish ACP places the right to follow a true conscience as its primary motivation for Church reform. Their objectives include:

1. Catholics are bound to follow their conscience on all moral issues, which means, people must put obeying the Gospel first, ahead of obeying the Church hierarchy.
2. All baptized people must be allowed to participate in all activities of the Church.

3. The administration of the Church must be reformed from a monarchical, hierarchical society to a society where all believers are treated as equals.
4. Local bishops and priests must relate to each other in a spirit of trust, support and generosity.
5. Liturgical celebrations must use rituals and language that are easily understood, inclusive and accessible to all.

These needed reforms necessarily involve a restructuring of the ministry where the gifts, wisdom and expertise of male and female ministers alike are incorporated in service to the community of faith. For this to happen, the governing system of the Church must be restructured from a power base to a service base. This would involve creating a culture of consultation and transparency in the appointment of Church leaders.

The ACP reminds us that the State and Church are separate entities with separate and distinct possibilities. The Church preaches the Gospel, while the State enacts laws for all the citizens.

Following the spirit of John XXIII and recognizing that the Spirit speaks through all peoples, the association wants a renewed relationship with fellow Christians and other faiths, even if not Christian.

The reformation of our beloved Church has begun. The *Documents of Vatican Council II* will serve as a blueprint for "our repentant journey to the well of Salvation." There is no need of a revolution where one side wins and the other loses. The truth will set us all free, and the truth is we will all help it happen.

CHAPTER XXVII

Vatican Council III: What Will Happen?

> *"It is not that the Gospel has changed: it is that*
> *we have begun to understand it better*
> *. . . and know that the moment has come to discern*
> *the signs of the time, to seize the opportunity*
> *and to look far ahead."*
>
> —John XXIII

"We want to be number 1 . . . but why and at what?"[1] Please excuse the political hyperbole. This is the mantra of President Obama and those who mirror his thinking in both parties of the United States as they urge us citizens to build, or educate, or cut the deficit, so that America can be number 1 again. We have a similar attitude in the Catholic Church, believing that Roman Catholicism is the perfect society and the only true Church in existence.

James Carroll wrote in his 2002 book *Toward a New Catholic Church: The Promise of Reform* that "the loss of credibility is destroying the very structure of the Church. Catholics have watched the priesthood collapse around harried men who still serve—while the Vatican rejects the service of married men and, most disturbingly, refuses to ordain women on the strictly fundamentalist ground that all of the apostles were men. . . . Why this crisis? Because [implicit in the Vatican's stance] virginal sexlessness is deemed morally superior to an actively erotic life—an inhuman idea that opens up a gap, an ethical abyss, into which the most well meaning of people can fall."[2]

While admitting that none of these factors taken alone led to the sexual abuse of children, Carroll's opinion is that the culture of silence, denial, dishonesty and the cover-up that accompanied those crimes makes it less likely for the Church, from the hierarchy to the people in the pew, to respond honestly and wisely.[3] Other authors feel that the cover-up by the hierarchy was motivated by a myth of Christian supremacy that goes back to the fourth century. Constantine, one of the most powerful Roman emperors, chose Byzantium as the capital of his empire in 324 AD and called it Constantinople. According to tradition, he became a patron of Christianity and helped spread Christianity throughout the empire, although he didn't become a Christian himself until shortly before his death in 337 AD. After his death the influence of Constantine on Christianity was missed.[4]

Before we discuss the how, and by whom, the reform of our beloved Catholic Church will now be executed, we the People of God must look back to Church history. As Edmund Burke said, "Those who don't learn from history are doomed to repeat it." The priest pedophile crisis is the third earth-shattering abuse of authority to hurt Christianity and Catholicism.

Father Martin P. Harney, a member of the Society of Jesus, wrote *The Catholic Church through the Ages,* an extensive history published in 1974. He reports on the first Church crisis in the Dark Ages, which is similar to the crisis we are experiencing worldwide today. He wrote, "The thousand years from Constantine's Catholicism to Luther's revolt was one long period of intellectual stagnation in which civilization and liberty were kept imprisoned in the darkness of ignorance and superstition by the tyrannical, obscurant and corrupt Catholic priesthood—popes, bishops, clerics and monks. No sensible Catholic denies the periods of intellectual retrogression in the course of those thousand years; such disasters are common in every civilization. Nor does he deny that there were many human failings in the Church's representatives during those centuries."[5]

Father Harney reports that the Church survived the *Dark Ages* of the tenth century, only to be challenged again by a process called

Lay Investiture in the eleventh century, whereby kings and civic rulers chose the Church hierarchy. He writes, "The roots of this conflict were the secular rulers' intrusions into the nomination of bishops and abbots and even popes. Bishoprics and abbeys, because of their feudal possessions, the main sources of their support, had become royal fiefs with vast regalia that were large castles, wide countrysides and even towns. . . . Under bad monarchs the door was opened to unholy ambition, bribery and the terrible sin of simony. As holders of these fiefs, the ecclesiastical lords exercised the same temporal rule over them as the lay lords over their fiefs. Like them too, the bishops and abbots were vassals of the king."

The consequences of investiture caused disruption in the clergy ranks, as "unprincipled clergymen offered enormous sums to obtain a bishopric or an abbey. To reimburse themselves, they sold minor benefices to clergy of lower rank. The evil traffic filled many higher and lower offices with unworthy clerics who, lost to the sense of their vocation, attempted marriage or brazenly lived in concubinage. A large number of the clergy thus defied a law binding in the Latin Church since the sixth century." Father Harney, a defender of the Church's traditional teachings, wrote, "But once again the gates of hell crashed in vain against the Rock of Peter." He could have added that once again the Catholic Church needed reformation to survive.[6]

Five popes participated in this needed reformation. Pope Leo IX gets credit for devising its methods. Pope Nicholas II restricted the election of popes to the cardinals alone, thus abolishing the emperor's nomination. This reform was called the Hildebrandine Reform after its chief activator Cardinal Hildebrand, who later was elected Pope Gregory VII, "one of the greatest of the popes."

The method by which the five popes effected this reform may now serve as a guideline for the People of God to initiate the reform of our beloved and broken Church in this the second millennium. According to Harney, "these popes held synods in almost every country of Western Europe and presided over them personally or by their legates. At these synods, by preaching a moral revival and by deposing simoniacal prelates, the popes labored for an ecclesiastical reform based on celibate clergy, elected without the use of money or violence, and inducted into office by the Church alone."[7]

I don't remember reading about the The Darkest Age or Lay Investiture while studying Church history in Ireland. I did learn about five great popes, like Gregory VII and Leo IX, who conducted ecclesiastical reform based on requiring clergy celibacy. Now I am asking myself if the exclusion of chapters on The Darkest Age and Lay Investiture by the hierarchy was intentional to protect the image of the Catholic Church as the perfect society.

What we Catholics have experienced since the early 1980s is another dark age in the church, where bishops and cardinals have chosen to live the myth that the Church is a perfect society "built on the Rock of Peter" while ignoring their own decrees of Vatican Council II.[8] Their failure to follow through on this Council's teachings is why we, the People of God, must stand up and demand that Vatican Council III be called. We cannot wait for the pope, the cardinals or the Curia to initiate a council. The manner in which the hierarchy and the Curia currently exercise their authority is a major cause of the crisis. The Documents of Vatican II will serve as a blueprint both for lay groups and clergy as they begin to repair the damage done to the Church.

Meanwhile, writers like Father Donald Cozzens believe that the Church will "submerge before any emergence" and that we might just be at the beginning of several generations of "darkness." He believes that this darkness is just one more of the Church's every-500-years-convulsions and that the central issue of this darkness is the misuse of authority within the Church. He forecasts a breakdown of the feudal system in the Church that has prevailed since the Middle Ages.[9]

For those of us who look for positive solutions to fix our broken Church, the first step will be a healing and reconciliation with the victims of sexual abuse and their families. And a second step would be an admission by the hierarchy that our Church is still a human society, capable of error, even though it was founded by Jesus Christ Son of God and guided by the Holy Spirit. Seeking forgiveness from the victims and their families, as Cardinal O'Malley did while visiting the Archdiocese of Dublin in 2010, will be effective in beginning the "repentant journey to the well of Salvation."[10]

By failing to report the crimes of pedophile priests to civil authorities, the hierarchy ignored their own guidelines contained in Paragraph 7 of the Council document *Declaration on Religious Freedom, Dignitatis Humanae*: "All men must be treated with justice and humanity. . . . Since civil society has the right to protect itself against abuses committed in the name of religious freedom, the responsibility of providing such protection rests especially with the civil authority. . . . These principles are necessary for the effective protection of the rights of all citizens and for the peaceful settlement of conflicts of rights." Many of the Church's hierarchy chose to ignore the rights of innocent children when they transferred the pedophile priests to another diocese or country to protect the good name of the Church.

What should we do first to prepare for Vatican Council III? I believe we should start by holding synods in every country throughout the Catholic world, just as the five popes did in reforming Catholicism in its "heroic eleventh century battles with kings for her freedom in the titanic struggles over *Lay Investiture*."[11] The theologians of the world should conduct conferences on the *Documents of Vatican Council II* at these synods, emphasizing to lay people their role and responsibility as reformers in their beloved but broken Church. Bishops who are invited as presenters at each synod should follow the example of Bishop Liam McDaid, who advised, "Jesus made no room in the Church for privilege, earthly pomp or power or lording over anyone."[12] The only power to be highlighted will be the power of the cross of Christ. As Athanasius of Alexandria said centuries ago, "The power of the cross has filled the world."[13]

Pope John Paul II laid the groundwork for Vatican Council III when he introduced the question of imperial power versus the message of St. Francis of Assisi "to follow the teachings of our Lord Jesus Christ and to walk in his footsteps." "Christians have often denied the Gospel, yielding to a mentality of power," John Paul confessed while addressing his congregation at his millennial Mass of Repentance on March 12, 2000.[14]

Following the national synods, diocesan synods will be organized using the personnel of the various reform groups who have been active in many countries of the Catholic World. Representatives of

- Associations of Catholic Priests;
- Corpus (one of the oldest reform groups, formed to promote a renewed Catholic Priesthood focused on the Eucharist to include married and single men and women priests);
- Voice of the Faithful (a reform group of fourteen thousand Catholics that was organized in the Archdiocese of Boston following Cardinal Law's mishandling of the priest pedophile crisis in the early eighties);
- Call to Action (a group that inspires and activates Catholics to act for justice and build inclusive communities through the lens of anti-racism and anti-oppression principles); and
- lay people from the parishes

will be invited to participate. Facilitators familiar with the *Documents of Vatican Council II* and with training in Process Mapping must run the meetings in the spirit of Resolution/Reform rather than Revolution. The local bishop or his representative would participate and lead the group in prayer, asking for both forgiveness and guidance from the Holy Spirit.

Some may argue that Vatican Council III has already begun in Ireland, Austria and the United States. The Association of Catholic Priests in Ireland meets regularly and has begun a dialogue with local bishops. Lay people participated and heard Father Kevin Hegarty quote from Howard Bleichner's *View from the Altar*, which describes the depth of the Church crisis in the United States and Ireland: "By any measure the sexual abuse scandals struck the Catholic Church in the U.S. with the force of a tsunami, dealing the worst blow in memory. Equally so in Ireland, the Ferns, Ryan, Murphy and Cloyne Reports in their cumulative and compelling detail highlight the acute level of dysfunction in the Church. . . . Church leadership seems divided and rudderless. Not since the eleventh century has there been such public disagreement among the bishops."[15]

As the diocesan synods progress, the pastors of local parishes will organize educational programs for both adults and teenagers in the local community. The diocesan Offices of Evangelization will supervise the parish programs, with a special emphasis on developing a clear understanding of the *Documents of Vatican Council II* and a study on the early Christian Church as recorded in the Acts of the Apostles. The atmosphere to be adopted at these meetings should be one of dialogue rather than an authoritative presentation on the Church's dogmatic teaching and papal encyclicals. The trained facilitator should be conscious that adult Catholics and young adults are aware of the need for reform in the hierarchy's attitude towards women, mandatory celibacy, ordination of married men and women, and in how authority in the Church is exercised. I visualize young people raising the question of why the Church is not consistent in its pro-life policies, punishing politicians who are pro-choice but ignoring politicians who are pro-war and pro-capital punishment. Facilitators should not be surprised if college students at the meeting ask, "When and where did all of the Church emphasis on power, secrecy and clericalism begin?"

The facilitators must be prepared to answer, "Will the windows of the Church be opened wide during Vatican Council III?" As historian and moralist Baron John Emerich Acton wrote in the last century, *"Power corrupts and absolute power corrupts absolutely."*

EPILOGUE

In a 2011 article in the *National Catholic Reporter*,[1] Father Richard P. McBrien, Crowley-O'Brien Professor of Theology at the University of Notre Dame and author, shares his perspective on why many older Catholics join *Call to Action* and *Voice of the Faithful*:

"Older Catholics—in their 60s, 70s, 80s and some few in their 90s—know what the pre-Vatican Church was like and how much better it became because of Pope John XXIII and the council he convened. That is why many of them have been disheartened by what they regard as a kind of retrenchment under Pope John Paul II and now Benedict XVI, and many of the bishops they appointed." He adds, "Many younger Catholics, at least those who care enough to remain more or less active in the Church, do not appreciate why so many older Catholics are so unhappy with the state of the Church today."

Just as other Catholic authors like Edward Jeep and Joseph Dillon emphasize the community aspect of the post-Vatican II Church in their book *Vatican II: A Promise Broken*,[2] McBrien writes, "The emphasis here is on the council's teaching that the Church is a *communion*—a communion between God and ourselves (the vertical dimension) and a communion of ourselves with one another in Christ by the power of the Holy Spirit (the horizontal dimension)."

He further explains, "Because the Church is a communion, its institutional structure is collegial rather than monarchical. . . . The Church is not a single international parish under the pastoral leadership of the Pope, subdivided into dioceses and parishes for administrative efficiency only . . . The Church is a communion of local Churches, or dioceses, each of which is the body of Christ, in its own particular place."

From 1979 to 1988 I was fortunate to serve as the pastor of St. Vincent Martyr Parish in Madison, New Jersey, where I experienced the true community of eighteen hundred families serving each other in unity "rooted in the presence and sanctifying activity of the Holy Spirit, manifested especially in the celebration of the Eucharist."[3]

For readers (lay or clergy) interested in learning how to make it all happen, I highly recommend Jeep and Dillon's *Vatican II: A Promise Broken*. The authors report on how their priest friend led the effort in bringing a community of faith to reality in two Tulsa, Oklahoma, parishes in spite of attempts by a conservative lay millionaire to torpedo the effort.

In democratic countries where the process of collaboration and dialogue with the opposition party is an integral part of governance, it should be relatively easy for the Church to increase collegiality among the hierarchy and create a collaborative atmosphere among all the "People of God." In his article McBrien reminds us that "the Church's mode of activity will necessarily differ from region to region. It will take longer, for example, in some regions of the world to accept a married clergy or the presence of women in positions of real pastoral authority than in other regions, such as our own."

It is my hope and prayer that the People of God, both lay and clergy, will join the Catholic reform organizations of the world, who hold the belief articulated by McBrien that it is "the Holy Spirit, not the hierarchy, not even the Pope, who governs the Church and leads it through all of human history to its final destiny in the kingdom of God."

The *Dogmatic Constitution on the Church in the Modern World, Lumen Gentium,* makes it clear that *aggiornamento* is absolutely vital: *"Today the human race is passing through a new age of its history. Profound and rapid changes are spreading by degrees around the world. Triggered by the intelligence and creative energies of man, these changes recoil upon him, upon his decisions and desires both individual and collective, and upon his manner of thinking and acting in respect to people and things. Hence we can already speak of a true social and cultural transformation, one with repercussions on man's religious life as well (LG 4)."*

I can hear Pope John XXIII repeating the phrase he frequently used as he convened Vatican Council II: *"It is time to open up the windows of the Church and let in some fresh air."*

SOURCES AND COMMENTS

Preface

1. James Carroll, *Toward a New Catholic Church* (New York: Mariner Books, 2002), 7.

I Vatican Council II: A Surprise

1. Maureen Sullivan, *Questions and Answers on Vatican Council II* (New York: Paulist Press, 2003), 17.
2. "I Choose John," *Time*, November 10, 1958.
3. Rembert G. Weakland, *A Pilgrim in a Pilgrim Church: Memoirs of a Catholic Archbishop* (Grand Rapids: William B. Eerdmans Publishing Co., 2009), 103.
4. Archbishop Marcel Lefebvre, "The Infiltration of Modernism in the Church," August 2, 2011. See at http://truecath.wordpress.com.
5. All citations of the Vatican II Documents come from Walter M. Abbott, Joseph Gallagher, eds., *The Documents of Vatican II With Notes and Comments by Catholic, Protestant, and Orthodox Authorities* (New York: Guild Press, 1966).
6. George Weigel, *Witness to Hope: The Biography of Pope John Paul II* (New York: Cliff Street Books/Harper Collins, 1999).

III   Vatican Council II: Third Session

1. Cf. *John* 18:37; *Matt.* 20:28; *Mark* 10:45. All further citations of the Bible come from the St. Joseph New Catholic Edition, Confraternity-Douay Version (New York: Catholic Book Publishing Co., 1962).
2. Elizabeth Cady Stanton and Susan B. Anthony were the founders of the National Women's Suffrage Association. In 1868 she and Anthony also founded *The Revolution,* a feminist magazine.
3. Margaret Sanger, who lived from 1879 to 1966, was the founder of Planned Parenthood.

V   New Definition of the Catholic Church

1. Janet E. Smith, *Humanae Vitae: A Generation Later,* Introduction to Smith's translation (Washington D.C.: CUA Press, 1991).
2. Peter Seewald, *Light of the World: The Pope, The Church and the Signs of the Times* (San Francisco: Ignatius Press, 2010).
3. David Gibson, "'The Catholic Church, Condoms and 'Lesser Evils,'" *New York Times,* November 27, 2010.

VI   Ireland before Vatican II

1. Russell Shorto, "The Irish Affliction," *New York Times Magazine,* February 9, 2011.
2. Dermot Keogh and Andrew McCarthy, *The Making of the Irish Constitution 1937* (Dublin: Mercier Press, 2007).
3. "The Leader Interview with Patrick Hederman, Abbot of Glenstal," *The Limerick Leader,* June 18, 2009.

VII   Child Abuse in Irish Institutions

1. Commission to Inquire into Child Abuse, *Report of the Commission to Inquire into Child Abuse* [*The Ryan Report*] (Dublin: The Stationery Office, 2009). The report is available on-line at http://www.childabusecommission.com/rpt/.

2. Tom Roberts, "Thousands of Children abused in Irish Institutions," *National Catholic Reporter,* May 29, 2009.
3. Commission of Investigation, *Report into the Catholic Archdiocese of Dublin* [*The Murphy Report*], July 2009, 1.15.
4. Congregation for the Doctrine of the Faith, *Crimen Sollicitationis, An Interpretation,* (Rome: Vatican Polyglot Press, 1962). Text available at http://www.vatican.va/resources/resources_crimen-sollicitationis-1962_en.html. See Glossary.
5. Roberts, "Thousands of Children."
6. BBC *Panorama, "Sex Crimes and the Vatican,"* September 30, 2006. For details, see written transcript at http://news.bbc.co.uk/2/hi/programmes/panorama/5402928.stm

VIII Father Marcial Maciel Degollado

1. Jason Berry, "Money paved way for Maciel's influence in the Vatican," *National Catholic Reporter,* April 6, 2010.
2. Jason Berry and Gerald Renner. "Breaking the Silence: Head of Worldwide Catholic Order Accused of History of Abuse," *Hartford Courant*, February 23, 1997.
3. Jason Berry, "Analysis: Legion of Christ Founder Leaves a Flawed Legacy," *National Catholic Reporter*, February 2, 2008.
4. Jason Berry and Gerald Renner, "New Sex Charge against Father Marcial: Sex-related case blocked in Vatican," *National Catholic Reporter,* December 7, 2001.
5. Ross Douthat, "The Better Pope," *New York Times*, April 11, 2010.
6. Jason Berry and Gerald Renner, "Breaking the Silence."
7. Ibid.
8. Ross Douthat, "The Better Pope."

IX Archbishop John Charles McQuaid and his Successors

1. John Cooney, "Cardinal Connell's actions were just 'too little, too late,'" *The Irish Independent,* November 23, 2009.

2. *Wikipedia*, "John Charles McQuaid: Early Life (1895-1914)." See at http://en.wikipedia.org/wiki/John_Charles_McQuaid.

3. John Cooney, *John Charles McQuaid: Ruler of Catholic Ireland,* (Cork: O'Brien Press, 1999).

4. Ibid.

5. *The Constitution of Ireland, Bunreacht na hEireann* (Enacted by the People of Ireland, July 1, 1937).

6. John Feeney, *John Charles McQuaid: the Man and the Mask* (Cork: Mercier Press, 1974), 78-79.

7. Cooney, *John Charles McQuaid, Ruler.*

8. Peadar Kirby, "Father Chris Mangan: Putting People First," *The Furrow* 40: no. 11 (1989): 643-650.

9. John Cooney, *John Charles McQuaid: Ruler.*

10. Francis Xavier Carty, *Hold Firm: John Charles McQuaid and the Second Vatican Council,* (Dublin: Columba Press, 2007).

11. Ibid.

X   Pope Benedict Offers Help to Ireland

1. Jody Corcoran, "Resign call to Cardinal after Euro400K payout," *The Irish Independent,* April 7, 2002.

2. Reverend Brian D'Arcy, *A Little bit of Healing in the Irish Catholic Church* (Lancaster, PA: Veritas, 2010).

3. A.W. Richard Sipe, "Secret sex in the celibate system," *National Catholic Reporter,* April 28, 2010.

4. Gerald Renner, "Bishop Admits Fathering Child," *Hartford Courant*, May 12, 1992.

5. David McKittrick, "A church in holy disorder," *The Irish Independent*, October 3, 1995.

6. Cian Molloy, "Irish bishops: abuse was prevalent in church culture," *National Catholic Reporter,* June 11, 2009.

7. Text of letter available at http://www.vatican.va/holy_father/benedict_xvi/letters/2010/documents/hf_ben-xvi_let_20100319_church-ireland_en.html.

8. Reverend Thomas Doyle, Expert testimony relating to Rev. James Jansen, Diocese of Davenport, June 18, 2007.

9. John Cooney, "'Surgeon's knife' has cut abuse evil from church, says new bishop," *The Irish Independent,* July 26, 2010.

10. Lisa Wangsness, "Church's song of sorrow has evolved and deepened," *Boston Globe*, February 20, 2011.

11. Paddy Agnew, "College president denies Irish seminary to close," *The Irish Times*, March 24, 2011.

12. Cahir O'Doherty, "Abuse survivors outrage at Vatican probe into Irish church sex abuse," *Irish Central*, June 10, 2010.

13. Michael Kelly, "Visitator to report that Irish church is near collapse, priest says," Catholic News Service, February 14, 2011.

14. John Cooney, "Priests hold hierarchy to account with 'union,'" *The Irish Independent*, July 29, 2010.

XI Archbishop Martin: A Breath of Fresh Air

1. Archbishop Diarmuid Martin, Address to the People of Ireland, November 26, 2009. Available at http://www.dublindiocese. ie/content/261109-archbishops-statement-publication-dublin-report.

2. Ibid.

3. Paddy Agnew, "Dismay in Vatican at negative Irish response to 'historic' meeting," *The Irish Times*, February 2, 2010.

4. John L. Allen, Jr., "Unexpected Praise for Irish Visitation," *National Catholic Reporter,* March 24, 2011.

5. Ibid.

6. Ibid.

7. Michael Kelley, "Radical shake-up for Maynooth," *The Irish Catholic*, March 24, 2011.

8. Tom Roberts, "Archbishop Martin renews call to examine culture that allowed sex abuse to happen," *National Catholic Reporter,* April 5, 2011.

9. Annysa Johnson, "Dublin archbishop urges church to reveal secrets," *JSOnline,* April 4, 2011.

XII   The Netherlands Embraces Vatican Council II

1. Reverend Robert Schreiter, "Theologian Schillebeeckx dies at 95," *National Catholic Reporter*, January 8, 2010.
2. The Congregation for the Clergy's response to the Dutch Pastoral Council, February 24, 1988.
3. Michael Gilchrist, "Growth of a 'New Church': a Dutch Experiment," *AD2000* 1: no. 4 (1988), 14.
4. Ralph McInerny, *What Went Wrong with Vatican II? The Catholic Crisis Explained* (Manchester, NH: Sophia Institute Press, 1998).
5. Gilchrist, "Growth."
6. Reported on Andere Tijden (Other Times), a VPRO television program.
7. F J. Bots, *Dutch Catholicism on the Eve of the Papal Visit* (Human Life International, 1985). Thanks to Father J. Bots S.J. Theologian/Sociologist, readers who want a detailed analysis of the causes and effects of the New Church in the Netherlands can read his analysis.

XIII   The Pope versus Belgium

1. John A. Dick, "Archbishop: church not obligated to compensate abuse victims," *National Catholic Reporter*, December 27, 2010.
2. Ibid.
3. Ibid.
4. Ibid.
5. John A. Dick, "Belgium archbishop's press officer calls it quits," *National Catholic Reporter*, November 3, 2010.
6. John A. Dick, "Belgian archbishop changes position on compensation for abuse victims," *National Catholic Reporter*, January 21, 2011.
7. Elisabetta Povoledo, "Bishop, 73, in Belgium Steps Down Over Abuse," *New York Times*, April 23, 2010.
8. Ibid.

9. Stephen Castle and Rachel Donadio, "Disgraced Bishop's Interview Stirs Outrage in Belgium," *New York Times*, April 15, 2011.

10. Philip Blenkinsop, "Belgian bishop admits he abused second nephew," Reuters, April 14, 2011.

11. Castle and Donadio, "Disgraced Bishop's Interview."

12. Ibid.

13. Ibid.

14. Ibid.

15. Ibid.

16. Rachel Donadio, Steven Castle and Jack Healy, "Vatican Criticizes Raid on Belgian Church Offices," *New York* Times, June 25, 2010.

17. Ibid.

18. Ibid.

19. Doreen Cavajal and Rachel Donadio, "Belgian Catholics Form Alternative Churches," *New York Times*, November 16, 2010.

20. Ibid.

21. Ibid.

22. Ibid.

23. Ibid.

XIV Australian Catholicism before and after Vatican II

1. Australian Bureau of Statistics, "Christianity in Australia, *Wikipedia* at http://en.wikipedia.org/wiki/Christianity_in_Australia.

2. Robert E. Dixon, *The Catholic Community in Australia* (Adelaide: Open Book Publishers, 2005).

3. Percival Serle, "John Joseph Therry", Dictionary of Australian Biography, 1949: Project Gutenberg Australia. See at http://gutenberg.net.au/dictbiog/0-dict-biogT-V.html.

4. Dixon, *The Catholic Community*.

5. Ibid.

6. "Kevin Rudd welcomes pilgrims to the World Youth Day opening mass," *The Australian*, July 15, 2008.

7. Chris McGillion, "Morale falters in the Australian Church," *National Catholic Reporter,* May 31, 2011.
8. Michael McKenna, "Temple Police Get their Man," *The Australian Catholic News*, May 7, 2011.
9. Ibid.
10. Ibid.
11. Ibid.
12. Tom Roberts, "Ousted bishop says he faced 'brick wall,'" *National Catholic Reporter,* May 13, 2011.
13. McGillion, "Temple Police."
14. Ibid.
15. The Synod of Oceania and *The General Secretariat of the Synod of Bishops,* Libreria Editrice Vaticana (1998).
16. McGillion, "Temple Police."
17. Ibid.
18. Damir Govorcin, "Bishop tells of 'terrifying' trip in a small boat," *Catholic Weekly,* September 4, 2011.
19. Ibid.

XV   The Universal Church and Germany Lag Behind

1. David Clohessy, Executive Director of SNAP, Blog, May 16, 2011.
2. Nicholas P. Cafardi, "Something Missing," *National Catholic Reporter,* July 17, 2010.
3. Peter Schneider, "Benedict's Fragile Church," *New York Times*, March 23, 2010.
4. Ibid.
5. Ibid.
6. Ibid.

XVI   Vatican Council II and Cardinal Ratzinger

1. Schneider, "Benedict's Fragile Church."
2. Ibid.

3. "Sex Scandal at Austrian Seminary," Associated Press, July 13, 2004.

4. David Willey, "Pope replaces sex scandal bishop," *BBC News*, October 7, 2004.

5. Richard Neuhaus, "Against Neoliberalism," *First Things*, August-September 2009.

6. Melinda Henneberger with James Sterngold, "Scandals in the Church: The Overview; Vatican Meeting on Abuse Issue Is Set to Confront Thorny Topics," *New York Times*, April 19, 2002.

7. Ibid.

8. *Ordinatio Sacerdotalis,* promulgated by Pope John Paul II on May 22, 1994, stating that "[the Church] holds that it is not admissible to ordain women to the priesthood, for very fundamental reasons" (Libreria Editrice Vaticana). See also: John Paul II in *Ordinatio Sacerdotalis,* c.f. Apostolic Exhortation *Christifideles Laici*, December 30, 1988, 31.

9. Kenneth Lanning, *Child Molesters: A Behavioral Analysis for Law Enforcement Officers*, (Third Edition, 2001).

XVII Four Popes: Who is the Winner?

1. Ross Douthat, "Better Pope."

2. Ibid.

3. Jason Berry, "Money paved way."

4. Robert J. Donovan, "'Never Again War,'" Pontiff's Appeal to U.N. Delegates," *Los Angeles Times*, October 5, 1965.

XVIII Roncalli: Student, Seminarian and Priest

1. Zsolt Aradi, James I. Tucek, and James C. O'Neill, *Pope John XXIII: An Authoritative Biography* (New York: Image/Doubleday, 1965), 26.

2. Ibid., 27.

3. Ibid., 41.

4. Ibid., 61.

5. Ibid., 103.

6. Angelo Giuseppe Roncalli, *In memoria di Monsignor Giacomo Maria Radini Tedeschi Vescovo di Bergamo,*" Società Editrice S. Alessandro, Bergamo, 1916.

XIX   Roncalli: Soldier to Archbishop and Diplomat

1. Aradi, Tucek and O'Neill, *Pope John* XXIII, 109.
2. Ibid., 113.
3. Ibid., 115.
4. Ibid., 235.

XX   Roncalli: Archbishop to Cardinal

1. Aradi, Tucek and O'Neill, *Pope John XXIII*, 169.
2. Ibid., 171.
3. Hatch, *A Man Named John: The Life of Pope John XXIII* (New York: Hawthorn Books, 1963), 74.
4. Ibid., 75.
5. Aradi, Tucek and O'Neill, *Pope John XXIII*, 197.
6. Ibid, 198.
7. Ibid., 204.
8. Ibid., 211.
9. Ibid., 220.
10. Ibid., 229.
11. Ibid.

XXI   Roncalli: Cardinal to Pope

1. Aradi, Tucek and O'Neill, *Pope John XXIII*, 237.
2. Ibid., 237-8.
3. Ibid., 239.
4. Ibid., 240.
5. Ibid., 241.
6. Ibid., 245.
7. Ibid., 260.
8. Hatch, *A Man Named John*, 132.

9.   Aradi, Tucek and O'Neill, *Pope John XXIII*, 290.
10. Ibid., 292.
11. Ibid., 299.

XXII What's Up with Conservatives?

1.   Thomas C. Fox, "St. Joseph diocese priest criticizes his bishop's leadership," *National Catholic Reporter*, September 15, 2009.
2.   Ibid.
3.   Joseph Cardinal Bernardin, "Called to be Catholic," Catholic Common Ground Project, August 12, 1996. Available at http://www.ewtn.com/library/BISHOPS/COMGROUN.HTM.
4.   Cardinal Bernard Law, "Response to 'Called to be Catholic,'" August 12, 1996. Available at http://www.ewtn.com/library/BISHOPS/COMGROUN.HTM.

XXIII Blessed John Paul: Awe and Ambivalence

1.   Nicole Winfield and Vanessa Gera, "John Paul's Sainthood Closer after Beatification," Associated Press, May 1, 2011.
2.   Pope Benedict XVI, "Papal homily during the liturgy at the Beatification of Pope John Paul II," Catholic Press, May 1, 2011.
3.   John L. Allen Jr., "In death as in life, John Paul a sign of contradiction," *National Catholic Reporter*, April 26, 2011.
4.   "US Catholics celebrate and debate the Pope's Legacy," Associated Press, April 29, 2011.
5.   John L. Allen, Jr., "Beatification of JP II: Interview with Cardinal Francis George," *National Catholic Reporter*, May 1, 2011.
6.   Joshua J. McElwee, Journalist, "Some question speed of John Paul II's beatification," *National Catholic Reporter*, February 2, 2011.
7.   Ibid.
8.   Ibid.
9.   Ibid.

10. NPR Staff, "Crowds Cheer as Pope Beatifies John Paul," *National Public Radio,* May 1, 2011.

11. John A. Allen, Jr., "Blessed John Paul II still stirs awe, ambivalence," *National Catholic Reporter,* May 13, 2011.

12. Ibid.

13. Ludmila and Stanislaw Grygiel, "Love is Possible," *Columbia* (Knights of Columbus), May 11, 2011.

14. Ibid.

15. Alton Pelowski, "Celebrating 30 years," *Columbia* (Knights of Columbus), April 29, 2011.

16. Ibid.

17. McElwee, "Some question."

18. Weigel, *Witness.*

XXIV The Challenge Facing Neo-Catholics

1. Alan Schreck, *Vatican II: the Crisis and the Promise* (Cincinnati, OH: St. Anthony's Press, Servant Books, 2005).

2. Ibid.

3. Michael Davies, *The Catholic Sanctuary and the Second Vatican Council* (Charlotte, NC: Tan Books, 2009).

4. Christopher A. Ferrara and Thomas E. Woods, *The Great Facade: Vatican II and the regime of novelty in the Roman Catholic Church* (Forest Lake, MN: The Remnant Press, 2002).

5. Schreck, *Vatican II.*

6. Michael Davies, *The Second Vatican Council and Religious Liberty* (Long Prairie, MN: Neumann, 1992).

7. Davies: *The Catholic Sanctuary.*

8. Ibid.

9. James Hitchcock, *Modernism's Limited Vision* (Princeton, NJ: Princeton University Press, 2002).

10. Schreck, *Vatican* II, 113-130.

11. Ibid.

12. Ibid., 58, 250, 260-261.

13. Ibid., 75-76.

14. Pope Benedict XVI. *The Ratzinger Report, An Exclusive Interview on the State of the Church* (The Catholic Company, June 1985), 24-25.
15. Pope John Paul II, *Final Report* of the 1985 Extraordinary Synod of Bishops, December 7, 1985, 44.

XXV Repairing Our Broken Church

1. Niall Dowd, "Arrest Bishop for Cover-up," *The Irish Voice* Editorial, August 24, 2011.
2. Paddy Clancy, "Disgraced Bishop Apologizes for Abuse," *The Irish Voice*, August 24, 2011.
3. Niall Dowd, "Arrest Bishop."
4. Ibid.
5. Ibid.
6. Thomas Doyle, "Report gives short shrift to Clericalism," *National Catholic Reporter*, June 10, 2011.
7. Ibid.
8. Taoiseach Enda Kenny, "Text of Irish prime minister's address on the Cloyne report," *National Catholic Reporter*, July 21, 2011.
9. Michael Kelly, "Prime Minister's harsh attack on Vatican wins praise in Ireland," *National Catholic Reporter*, August 3, 2011. See at NCRonline.org/node/25821.
10. Iggy O'Donovan, "People Not Going to Confession Anyway," *The Drogheda Independent*, July 20, 2011.
11. Reverend Thomas Doyle, "A Very Short History of Clergy Sexual Abuse in the Catholic Church." See at http://www. crusadeagainstclergyabuse.com/htm/AShortHistory.htm
12. Thomas Doyle, "Unless the Catholic hierarchy examines its obsession with power it cannot reform itself," *The Irish Times*, July 16, 2011.

XXVI Resolution and Reform versus Revolution

1. Cardinal Christoph Schönborn, Address to the Austrian Priests' Initiative, Catholic News Service, August 10, 2010.
2. Christa Pongratz-Lippitt, "Push for reform grows in Austria." *National Catholic Reporter*, September 16, 2011.
3. See The Schönborn Site at http://www.cardinalschönborn.com/bio.html.
4. Christa Pongratz-Lippitt, "Push for reform grows."
5. Ibid.
6. Ibid.
7. Bishop Liam McDaid, Address to the Congregation on the day of his installation as Bishop of Clogher, Ireland, *The Irish Independent,* May 7, 2010.
8. Report on meeting of Clogher ACP. See at http://www.associationofcatholicpriests.ie/2011/09/report-on-meeting-of-clogher-acp/.

XXVII Vatican Council III: What Will Happen?

1. David J. Rothkopf, "Redefining the Meaning of No. 1," *New York Times*, October 8, 2011.
2. Carroll, *Toward a New Catholic Church*, 8.
3. Ibid.
4. Martin P. Harney, *The Catholic Church through the Ages* (Boston: The Daughters of St. Paul, 1974)
5. Ibid.
6. Ibid., 123.
7. Ibid., 124.
8. Ibid.
9. Mary Jo Dangel, "Father Donald Cozzens: How to build a Better Church, *St. Anthony Messenger,* February 2006.
10. McDaid, Address.
11. Harney, *The Catholic Church.*
12. McDaid, Address.

13. St. Athanasius the Great, the 20th bishop of Alexandria, (328-373 AD).
14. Pope John Paul, Address to the People of Jordan, March 12, 2000.
15. Howard P. Bleichner, *View from the Altar: Reflections on the Rapidly Changing Priesthood* (New York: The Crossroads Publishing Co., 2004).

Epilogue

1. Richard McBrien, "The church is a communion of local churches," *National Catholic Reporter*, August 8, 2011.
2. Edward Jeep and Joseph Dillon, *Vatican II: A Promise Broken* (Charleston, SC: Skeehan Project, 2010).
3. McBrien.

APPENDIX

APOSTOLIC NUNCIATURE
IN IRELAND
N. 808/97

Dublin, 31 January 1997

Strictly confidential

Your Excellency,

The Congregation for the Clergy has attentively studied the complex question of sexual abuse of minors by clerics and the document entitled "Child Sexual Abuse : Framework for a Church Response", published by the Irish Catholic Bishops' Advisory Committee.

The Congregation wishes to emphasize the need for this document to conform to the canonical norms presently in force.

The text, however, contains "procedures and dispositions which appear contrary to canonical discipline and which, if applied, could invalidate the acts of the same Bishops who are attempting to put a stop to these problems. If such procedures were to be followed by the Bishops and there were cases of eventual hierarchical recourse lodged at the Holy See, the results could be highly embarrassing and detrimental to those same Diocesan authorities.

In particular, the situation of 'mandatory reporting' gives rise to serious reservations of both a moral and a canonical nature".

Since the policies on sexual abuse in the English speaking world exhibit many o the same characteristics and procedures, the Congregation is involved in a global study of them. At the appropriate time, with the collaboration of the interested Episcopal Conferences and in dialogue with them, the Congregation will not be remiss in establishing some concrete directives with regard to these Policies.

To: the Members of the Irish Episcopal Conference
    - their Dioceses

For these reasons and because the abovementioned text is not an official document of the Episcopal Conference but merely a study document, I am directed to inform the individual Bishops of Ireland of the preoccupations of the Congregation in its regard, underlining that in the sad cases of accusations of sexual abuse by clerics, the procedures established by the Code of Canon Law must be meticulously followed under pain of invalidity of the acts involved if the priest so punished were to make hierarchical recourse against his Bishop.

Asking you to kindly let me know of the safe receipt of this letter and with the assurance of my cordial regard, I am

Yours sincerely in Christ,

+ *(signature)*
+Luciano Storero
Apostolic Nuncio

GLOSSARY

Aggiornamento—an Italian word, etymologically it means 'bringing up to date', revitalizing.

Annus Horribilis—attributed to the British Queen, Elizabeth, after the tragic death of Princess Diane. Translated . . . a horrible year.

Apostolic Visitor—a church official, empowered to represent the Pope in countries that don't have diplomatic relations with the Vatican.

Assumption—refers to the Catholic belief or dogma that Mary the mother of Jesus was assumed body and soul into heaven at her death. The feast is celebrated on August 15 annually.

Benedictines (Order)—a community of priests, brothers and religious sisters founded by St. Benedict. He wrote the rule of the order that is still being observed today.

Biretta—a hard, square ceremonial hat worn by the Roman Catholic clergy.

Bishops: Episcopal Order—governed by bishops.

> *Synod of Bishops*—a coming together of bishops for an international or national meeting.

> *College of Bishops*—the group of bishops given the legal status of an ecclesiastical corporation.

BishopAccountability.org—an organization formulated in 2003 to document the sexual abuse crisis by Catholic clergy in the Roman Catholic Church.

Cardinal—from "cardo," the Roman word for hinge. Cardinals were hinge men. They were appointed by the popes as envoys to other dioceses or countries when delegates of the Vatican were needed to make local decisions.

Canon Law—a body of laws and regulations adopted in 1983 by ecclesiastical authority to outline jurisdiction in the Catholic Church.

Canon Lawyer—a priest or layperson with expertise in Canon Law.

Caritas International—a confederation of 165 Catholic relief, development and social services organizations operating in over 200 countries worldwide.

Church: *pre-Vatican II*—the pope, Curia, bishops and priests.

> *post-Vatican II*—all the People of God (pope, cardinals, bishops and laity).

Conclave (Papal)—a meeting of the College of Cardinals convened during a period of vacancy in the papal office to elect a bishop of Rome, who then automatically becomes pope.

Charismatic Renewal—a Catholic religious group or movement of individuals that features prayer meetings, vibrant Masses, speaking in tongues and healing by divine intervention.

Consistory—a place of assembly where a church council or papal senate met.

Christian Dialogue—an interchange and discussion between members of two or more Christian church members for the purpose of mutual understanding or harmony. The long term goal is Christian Unity.

Clericalism—a derogatory term describing the power of the clergy or principals who favored the same.

The Concilium—a worldwide journal of theology founded in 1965 in the Netherlands with the mission of assisting churches and spiritual communities committed to hope, love, justice and peace on earth.

Council Fathers—the cardinals, archbishops, bishops and Periti who participated in Vatican Council II

Crimen Sollicitationis—instructions published in 1962 by the Vatican, over the signature of Pope John XXIII, outlining a policy of strictest security in dealing with allegations of sexual abuse by priests and threatening those who spoke out with excommunication. This document was revised in 2001 by Cardinal Ratzinger.

Curia—the administrative body of the Roman Catholic Church consisting of various departments functioning under the authority of the Pope.

Divine Office—the psalms, readings and prayers used by religious at the canonical hours.

Dominican (Order) – a community of priests, brothers and religious sisters who live and work in community according to the rule of their founder St. Dominic.

Eparch—a ruling bishop in the Eastern Byzantine Church.

Exarch—the supreme head of the independent Orthodox Church in Bulgaria.

Exarchate—the position, rank or province of an exarch.

Evangelization—preaching the gospel for the purpose of converting people to Christianity.

Holy See—an alternative phrase to designate the papal household.

Holy Year—a year of jubilee celebrated throughout the Catholic world at the discretion of the pope.

Infallibility, Infallible—designations that the pope is incapable of error when he teaches *ex cathedra* (in his official capacity) on faith and morals.

Lay Formation—education and training of lay members (not clergy) in the Church to serve as leaders, trustees, administrators and evangelizers of the teachings of Jesus Christ.

Lay investiture—the appointment of bishops, abbots and other church officials by feudal lords or vassals.

Legion of Christ, members called ***Legionaries***—a conservative religious order founded in 1941 by Father Marcial Marciel Degollado, who was accused by former seminarians of molesting them. He was also accused of fathering three children with two different women.

Liberation Theology—a theology used as means of freeing people from social, economic or political oppression or injustice

Magisterium—the Catholic Church's teaching authority, vested in the bishops as successors of the apostles, under the Roman Pontiff as successor of St. Peter.

Mandatum—an authoritative order entrusting the recipient as a trustworthy teacher of Catholic doctrine.

Marriage and Family Life Movement—a ministry that offers practical help and advice to strengthen marriages and families through conferences, lectures and self help groups.

Mental Reservation—a qualification (of a statement) that one makes to himself/herself but does not express.

Missal—a large book containing all the prayers, readings and rubrics authorized by the Catholic Church for the celebration of Mass or a small version used by lay people who participate in the Mass.

Modernism—an attempt to redefine traditional teachings, dogmas and beliefs in the light of modern science. It was condemned by the Roman Catholic Church in 1907 as a denial of the faith.

Modus Operandi—the manner of operating.

Natural Law—the rules of conduct inherent in every human person, created by God, can be discovered by reason as they are based on man's innate moral sense.

Neo-Catholic—a term created in 2002 by two conservative Catholic authors to describe progressive Catholics who embraced a theology and ideology based on the Documents of Vatican Council II, in contrast to the pre-Vatican II traditional mindset.

Nuncio—a prelate (cardinal or bishop) that represents the pope to a foreign government.

Novitiate—a place where aspirants to a religious order live, work and pray.

O.F.M. (Ordo Fratrum Minorum)—members of the Franciscan Order, who follow the original rule of their founder St. Francis of Assisi. The order was founded in 1209.

Orthodox Eastern Church—distinguished from the Western Latin Rite Church, and consists of four patriarchates in Eastern Europe.

People of God—a redefinition of the Church by Vatican Council II to include all of the laity and not just the pope and hierarchy as it was defined in the pre-Vatican II era.

Piacenza Family—a wealthy Italian family with several nuns and priests.

Polenta—an Italian dish made of cornmeal.

The Pope's titles—Holy Father, Roman Pontiff, Vicar of Christ, who Catholics believe is Christ's earthly representative ruling the Church.

Process Mapping—a technique whereby a <u>business process</u> or workflow is converted into a visual, step-by-step diagram. Process mapping is used to better understand an existing process and to help develop a more effective one. The goal of process mapping is to improve organizational results.

Prothonotary Apostolic—a title given to seven members of the College of Prothonotaries Apostolic, who record important pontifical events.

Psychosexual Fixation—a syndrome attached to a theory that individuals may have the growth of their sexual development arrested psychologically by a trauma or premature sexual experience in their childhood.

Reformation—the sixteenth century religious movement that aimed at reforming the Catholic Church and resulted in establishing the Protestant churches.

Rites of the Catholic Church—Eastern and Western (Latin), each with its own unique liturgy and other rites.

Secretariat of State—an administrative staff or department of the Vatican.

SNAP—the survivors' network of those sexually abused by priests.

Tonsure—a clipping or shaving of part of the hair of the head as a formal sign of entering the clerical or monastic state. Traditionally interpreted as symbolizing Christ's crown of thorns.

Transubstantiation—the act of changing the substance of bread and wine into the substance of the body and blood of Christ during the celebration of Mass.

Universal Church—the original name of the Roman Church in the second century. Used today to describe all of the Catholic faithful of the world.

Western Schism or *Papal Schism*—a split within the Catholic Church from 1378 to 1417. It was driven by politics rather than any theological disagreement. The Schism was ended by the Council of Constance (1414-1418).

WEORC—an association of priests, religious women and men who have moved from full ministry in the Catholic Church to other work. The members of WEORC act as a network to assist others who are making similar transitions. WEORC is an of English form of the word "Work"

Worker Priests—an initiative by the French Church for priests to take up work in places like car factories to experience the everyday life of the working class.

FINBARR M. CORR ED. D

He served as a Catholic Priest for twenty-eight years in the Diocese of Paterson, N.J.

As a licensed Marriage and Family therapist for thirty-three years in New Jersey he provided counseling through Partners in Change Inc, a company he founded in 1989.

He created a student assistance program for Catholic high schools and grammar schools in northern New Jersey and later taught Psychology at community colleges for ten years.

For forty years he has been an active participant in dialoging with other Christian Faiths, with the goal of facilitating Christian Unity. As a Rotarian he initiated a dialogue with moderate Muslims in N.J. and for five years facilitated (with fellow Rotarians) a dialogue with moderate Muslims who live and work on Cape Cod.

He authored the following books>

A Kid from Legaginney
Bridges from Legaginney
Living Laughing and Loving Thru Marriage
Up Close and Personal: Talking with Teens and Parents
The Many Loves of Joe Carroll (a memoir)